THE ART OF WAR

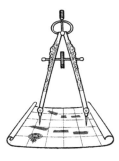

THE ART OF WAR
WAR AND
MILITARY THOUGHT

Martin van Creveld

General Editor: John Keegan

CASSELL&CO

For COLONEL MOSHE BEN DAVID, *student and friend*

'From knowledge to competence it is a big step; from ignorance to competence, a bigger one still.'
HANS VON SEECKT

Cassell & Co
Wellington House, 125 Strand
London WC2R 0BB

First published 2000
Reprinted 2000

British Library Cataloguing-in-Publication Data
A catalogue record for this book is available from the British Library.
ISBN 0-304-35264-0

Cartography: Arcadia Editions
Picture research: Elaine Willis
Design: Martin Hendry
Printed in Italy by Printer Trento S.r.l.

Typeset in Monotype Sabon

ACKNOWLEDGEMENTS

Forming part of the Cassell illustrated History of Warfare series, this volume was planned in consultation with the general editor, John Keegan, and the then publishing director at Weidenfeld & Nicolson, Judith Flanders. With them I decided to keep it free of references so as to retain as much as possible of the limited space available for the text proper. The reader who is interested in pursuing the topic further, however, will find a list of reading at the end. In this way, it is to be hoped, the demands of both brevity and scholarship can be reconciled.

MARTIN VAN CREVELD
Potsdam

The siege of Antwerp, culminating in its capture on 17 August 1585 by Alexander Farnese, the Duke of Parma.

Contents

❧ ⊹—◦◦O◦◦—⊹ ❧

KEY TO MAPS

Military units—size

XXXXX
army group

XXXX
army

XXX
corps

XX
division

X
brigade

III
regiment

II
battalion

Military movements

attack

retreat

air attack

battle

fortress

Geographical symbols

urban area

road

railway

river

seasonal river

canal

border

bridge or pass

MAP LIST

CHRONOLOGY

BC

453–221	Period of the Warring States (China).
c. 400	Sun Tzu writes *The Art of War*, one of the best works on war ever written.
371	Spartan hegemony broken at the battle of Leuctra.
mid third century	Work of Aeneas the Tactician.
334–323	Alexander's campaigns.
210	Han dynasty unifies China.
146	Fall of Carthage and of Corinth; Roman rule now extends over the entire Mediterranean.
first century	Asclepiodotus writes an *Outline of Tactics*.
29	Battle of Actium; Roman Empire definitely established.

AD

mid first century	Onasander writes *The General*.
late first century	Frontinus writes *Strategemata*.
c. 117	Roman Empire reaches its greatest extent.
late fourth century	Vegetius writes *Epitoma Rei Militaris*, the best work ever written on Roman military organization and tactics.
476	Fall of the Western Roman Empire.
535–567	Campaigns of Belisarius and Narses.
late sixth century	*Strategikon* attributed to Emperor Maurice.
800	Charlemagne crowned Emperor of Rome.
late ninth century	*Tacticon* attributed to Emperor Leo (the Wise).
1096	Start of the First Crusade.
1291	Last crusader foothold in Palestine lost.
1336–1453	Hundred Years War.
1348	Battle of Crécy. First recorded use of gunpowder in battle.
1400	Honoré Bonet writes *The Tree of Battles*.
1410	Christine de Pisan writes *The Art of Chivalry*.
1453	Fall of Constantinople to the Ottomans.
1492	Spanish *reconquista* completed with the fall of Granada.

1492	Columbus reaches Hispaniola.
1494	Beginning of the French–Spanish–Austrian struggle for Italy.
1494	Vasco da Gama reaches India by sea.
1520–21	Machiavelli writes *The Art of War*.
1522	First use of the 'Italian system' of fortification.
1566	Beginning of the Dutch Revolt.
1571	Ottoman naval power broken in the battle of Lepanto.
1584	Maurice of Nassau assumes command of the Dutch army at the struggle against Spain.
1588	Spanish Armada defeated.
1618–48	Thirty Years War.
1625	Grotius publishes *The Law of War and Peace*.
1632	Gustavus Adolphus killed at Luetzen.
1639–43	Montecuccoli writes *Treatise on War*.
1643	Battle of Rocroi breaks Spanish power and lays the foundation for French hegemony in Europe.
1702–14	War of the Spanish Succession.
1705–6	Vauban publishes *The Attack and Defence of Places*.
1712	Battle of Poltava marks the triumph of Russia over Sweden and the rise of the former to the status of a great power.
1720s	Folard writes *A History of Polybios*.
1720s	Puysegur, attempting to adapt Vauban's system to field warfare, writes *The Art of War by Principles and Rules*.
1732	De Saxe writes *Mes Rêveries*, expounding eighteenth-century warfare at its best.
1741–63	Campaigns of Frederick the Great.
1756–63	Seven Years War leads to the conquest by Britain of India and Canada.
1770	Guibert writes *General Essay on Tactics*, pointing the way to the military system of the French Revolution.
1776–83	War of the American Revolution.
1780s	'Strategy' invented.
1789	Start of the French Revolution.

1792	War of the First Coalition; the *levée en masse* proclaimed.	1914–18	First World War.
1796–9	Berenhorst publishes *Reflections on the Art of War*, pointing out the importance of moral factors.	1915	Invention of the tank.
		1917	Russian Revolution.
1799	Buelow publishes *Spirit of the Modern System of War*. Invents 'bases' and 'lines of communication'.	1921	Douhet publishes *The Command of the Air*, probably the most important book on the subject ever written.
1800	Battle of Marengo illustrates the power of '*la manoeuvre sur les derrières*'.	1922	Fuller publishes *Lectures on Field Service Regulations III*, laying the foundations of armoured warfare.
1805–6	Jomini publishes *A Treatise on Grand Operations of War*, presenting strategy as a question of moving forces in two-dimensional space.	1927	Lawrence publishes *The Seven Pillars of Wisdom*, expounding guerrilla tactics.
1813	Battle of Leipzig marks the height of the Napoleonic Wars.	1929	Liddell Hart publishes *The Decisive Wars of History*, which is later to turn into his celebrated work *Strategy*.
1815	Battle of Waterloo puts an end to French Revolutionary and Napoleonic Wars.	1930s	Term 'grand strategy' invented.
1832	Clausewitz's *On War* published posthumously by his widow. Quickly gains fame as 'a treasure of the human spirit'; probably the greatest Western work on war ever written.	1935	Germany builds the first armoured divisions.
		1936	Ludendorff publishes *The Nation at War*.
		late 1930s	Mao's writings on people's war.
		1939–45	Second World War.
1854–6	Crimean War.	1941	German attack on the USSR initiates largest single military campaign ever known.
1859	Franco-Austrian war.		
1860s	Du Picq writes *Battle Studies*, focusing on the behaviour of men in battle.	1941	Japanese attack on Pearl Harbor.
		1945	Nuclear weapons dropped on Hiroshima and Nagasaki.
1861–5	American Civil War. Witnesses first large-scale use of railways, telegraph and breech-loading rifles.	1949	USSR explodes nuclear device.
		1949	Chinese Revolution triumphs.
		1950–53	Korean War.
1866	Prusso-Austrian war witnesses the triumph of the General Staff.	1953	US tests first hydrogen bomb.
		1958	Soviet Union explodes largest nuclear device known to date.
1870–71	Franco-Prussian war establishes German hegemony in Europe.		
1880	Mahan publishes *The Influence of Seapower upon History, 1660–1783*. Advocates command of the sea as a route to national greatness.	*c.* 1960	First intercontinental ballistic missiles (ICBM) become operational, turning any idea of defending against a nuclear attack into nonsense.
		1963–75	Vietnam War shows limits of US military power.
1893	The Schlieffen Plan conceived.	1966	Schelling publishes *Arms and Influence*.
1898	Spanish–American war.	1967	China tests nuclear device.
1904–5	Russo-Japanese war.	1971	Largest, and last, Indo-Pakistani war.
1911	Corbett publishes *Some Principles of Maritime Strategy* in opposition to Mahan.	1972	Strategic Arms Limitation Treaty (SALT) signed.
		1973	Largest, and last, Arab–Israeli War.
1911	Italian–Turkish war sees first military use of aircraft.	1982	Falklands War.
		1991	Gulf War.
1912	Overthrow of the Chinese Ch'ing dynasty; establishment of a republic.	1991	Following its defeat in Afghanistan, the Soviet Union disintegrates. Some claim history has come to an end.

STUDYING WAR

THE EARLIEST MILITARY RECORDS *were not theoretical treatises but accounts of deeds done. The destruction of the city of Khamanu, Elam, by the Assyrian king Ashurbanipal, is shown here in stone relief,* c. 649 BC.

INTRODUCTION

THE ORIGINS OF military thought are unknown. Since war is among the oldest of human activities, and long antedates the invention of writing, presumably the earliest attempts to think it out have not survived and took the form of poems which were sung or recited on suitable occasions. We do in fact know that many tribal societies have warlike songs. Composed by anonymous bards and often modified to fit subsequent events as they unfold, their purpose is to record glorious deeds that took place in the past, encourage the warriors on one's own side and frighten the enemy. And indeed the Homeric poems, like broadly similar ones in other cultures, appear to have originated in just such a collection of songs.

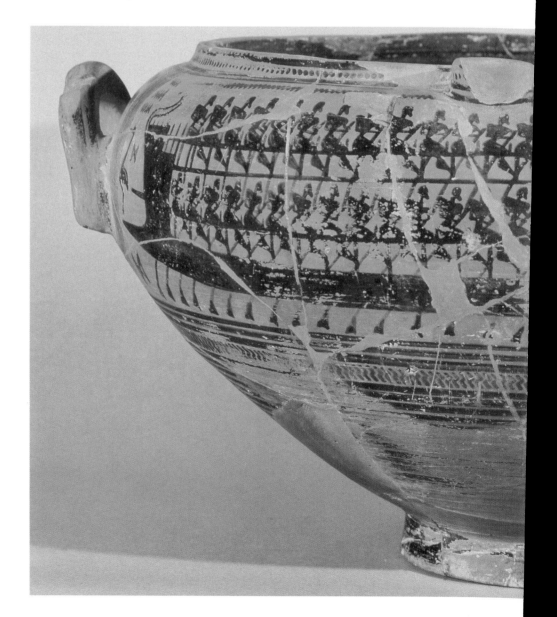

However revealing and inspiring, poems are no substitute for military theory. This volume, concentrating on systematic attempts to understand the nature of war and the ways in which it ought to be fought, will present the reader with a brief survey of the development of military thought from its origins to the present day. I have decided to make my survey wide rather than deep, the objective being less to analyse a few 'great' writers – each of whom has been discussed many times – and more to aim at a measure of comprehensiveness and, above all, show continuity of thought. Even so, given the very limited space available, some concessions have had to be made. Obviously only a small selection of those who have turned their minds to the study of war could be included. The rest, particularly the enormous number who have done so since 1945, will have to excuse me if I allow their writings to speak for themselves.

In this connection the vexed question as to whether and how theory

An amphora showing men rowing a warship, late eighth century BC. *This is possibly how the ships that carried the Greek army to Troy may have looked.*

MISSILE-THROWING
WEAPONS

The earliest known military theory was written down in around 400 BC, in China, just at the time when the first stone-throwing machines were being invented in Greece. During the period covered in this book military theory and military technology advanced together.

influenced action will be largely put aside. At a conference I once attended, one speaker claimed that American 'decision-makers' of the Second World War – meaning senior civil servants and generals with research money to spend – treated the social scientists from whom they deigned to commission studies 'as dogs treat lamp-posts'. Upon examination it turned out that one of the social scientists in question happened to be named Ruth Benedict. Her study of Japanese culture, written in 1943–4 and later published under the title *The Chrysanthemum and the Sword*, may or may not have actually influenced any particular decision made

MEDIEVAL CATAPULT

EIGHTEENTH-CENTURY ARTILLERY AND SUPPORT TEAM

TWENTIETH-CENTURY 'TOWED' ARTILLERY AND TEAM

TWENTIETH-CENTURY ARMOURED SELF-PROPELLED ARTILLERY

during the war – in fact it would be very difficult to tell. More important, though, having sold by the hundreds of thousands, it did more to shape Western, American in particular, notions about Japan than almost any other work before or since, despite the fact that at the time she wrote her study Benedict had never been to Japan, nor did she know Japanese. Certainly it did more than the vast majority of decision-makers whose very names, moderately well known in their own time, have since been forgotten; and many of whom would probably have been unable to put whatever ideas they had about Japan in coherent form even if they had wanted to.

The outline of this volume is as follows. Chapter 1 deals with the ancient Chinese military thinkers. Chapter 2 presents a brief outline of classical,

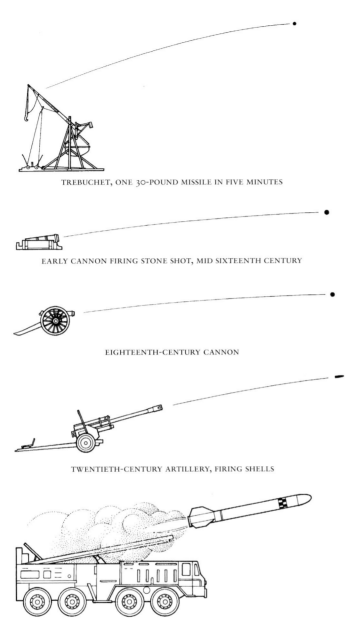

TREBUCHET, ONE 30-POUND MISSILE IN FIVE MINUTES

EARLY CANNON FIRING STONE SHOT, MID SIXTEENTH CENTURY

EIGHTEENTH-CENTURY CANNON

TWENTIETH-CENTURY ARTILLERY, FIRING SHELLS

LATE TWENTIETH-CENTURY MISSILE LAUNCHER

MISSILE PROJECTION

The original ballistae *had a range of approximately 300 metres, against thousands of miles for modern missiles. From Sun Tzu to Thomas Schelling, military theory was profoundly influenced by these changes.*

Byzantine and Western medieval military thought. Chapter 3 covers the period between 1500 and the end of the Seven Years War, and chapter 4 the immediate forerunners of Jomini and Clausewitz as well as those writers themselves. Chapter 5 discusses the rest of the nineteenth century to 1914, and chapter 6 deals with Mahan and Corbett as the only two writers on the theory of naval warfare (not to be confused with its history, on which there are many fine works) who are worth studying. Chapter 7 analyses the period between the two world wars, including air warfare, armoured warfare, the indirect approach and total warfare. Finally, chapter 8 outlines some of the debates about war that have taken place since 1945, focusing on both nuclear strategy and modern guerrilla warfare.

CHAPTER ONE

CHINESE MILITARY THOUGHT

DURING THE TIME that the Chinese classical military writings were produced, chariots were giving way to cavalry. Bronze statues of horsemen, Han dynasty, 206–220 BC.

CHINESE MILITARY THOUGHT

Han dynasty statuette of a warrior, c. 210 BC.

A S ALREADY INDICATED in the Introduction, the earliest known writings on the subject of war did not constitute theoretical treatises. Instead they took the form of narratives: either poems that had been written down – such as the Epic of Gilgamesh and the Homeric poems – or prose accounts commemorating individual campaigns and battles such as may be found inscribed on ancient Egyptian, Babylonian and Assyrian monuments. Both prose accounts and poems were intended to record and glorify events which may or may not have been historical but which, even in the case of the Epic of Gilgamesh with its array of gods and godlike heroes, may have contained some kernel of truth. In addition, the poems in particular served the purpose of inspiring the young to deeds of excellence.

In China, which is where our survey must start, a third type of writing on war developed and enjoyed prominence. China after the fall of the Chou (*c.* 400 BC) was divided into a large number of warring principalities. Fighting each other tooth and nail, these principalities developed standing professional armies as well as expert generals. Between about 400 and 200 BC several of these generals appear to have put their methods down in writing; alternatively they

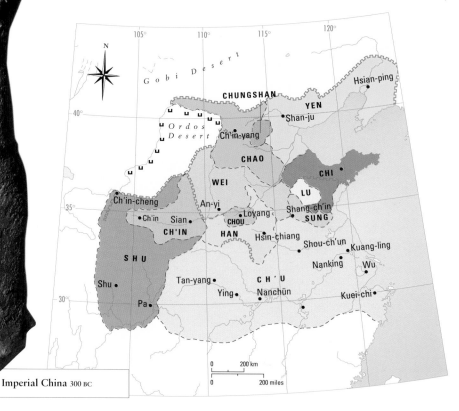

Imperial China 300 BC

had various texts, written by others, attributed to them by way of enhancing those texts' authority. In some cases, including that of Sun Tzu as the greatest of their number, it is possible that the generals themselves were not historical figures but merely legendary pegs on which anonymous authors hung their own thoughts. This method is still often used in China today. To make your case, don't stress your originality, as many a modern Westerner would do; but, on the contrary, attribute what you are saying to somebody who lived long ago and whose fame is greater than yours.

Once composed or written, both martial poems and prose accounts of war constituted public possessions which were recited, read, or even displayed by being inscribed on stone. Not so the Chinese texts, which, precisely because they claimed to lay bare the methods which famous generals used in order to gain their victories, were treated as state secrets. Their nature is evident from their names: 'Ta'i Kung's Six Secret Teachings', 'The Methods of the Ssu-ma', 'Three Strategies of Huang Shih-kung' and the 'Military Methods' attributed to Sun Pin. All these, as well as several others, were the product of the period of the warring principalities. They tended to disappear into royal archives where they were made available to the elect; there, given that they were written on strips of bamboo and joined together by having strings passed through holes in them, there was plenty of occasion for them to fall into disorder. Only during medieval (Sung) times were seven of the surviving texts copied or printed on silk and disseminated, serving as textbooks on which the annual

WARRING STATES TO THE UNIFICATION OF CHINA AND THE GROWTH OF THE CH'IN STATE

Sun Tzu is credited with holding back the expansion of the Ch'in state for a number of years. His military experiences in these operations formed the basis for his military treatise The Art of War.

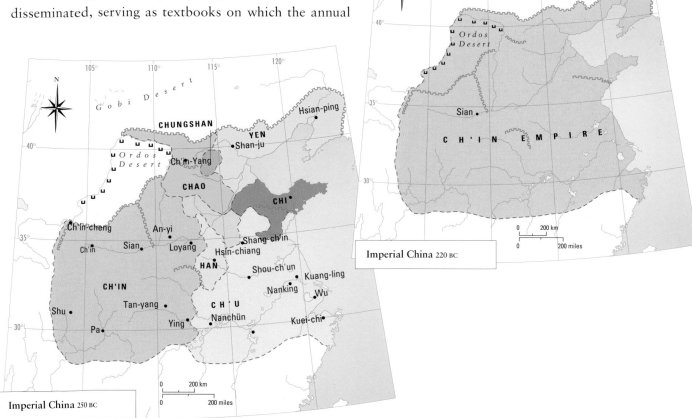

Imperial China 220 BC

Imperial China 250 BC

LEFT: *Early Chinese emperors sometimes went to their graves with entire armies, made of terracotta, to accompany them in the afterworld. The one shown here was made for Emperor Ch'in Shih Huang Ti (259–210 BC) and excavated following its chance discovery in Xi'an, Shaanxi Province, in March 1974.*

RIGHT: *A Ch'in dynasty figure of a warrior from Emperor Ch'in Shih Huang Ti's Terracotta Army. This is how a general in the time of Sun Tzu may have looked.*

military examinations were based. One, by Sun Pin, disappeared altogether and only came back to light in 1972 when a Han tomb was opened and a copy of it was discovered.

Some of the texts that have come down to us are presented in the form of lectures given by commanders to rulers into whose employ they wanted to enter. Wu Tzu, for example, persuaded the Marquis of Wei to listen to what he had to say, and, while seated on a mat with a glass of wine, he opened his exposition. Other texts consist of short, pungent phrases which had come down from, or else were attributed to, some outstanding general and were then surrounded by the comments of others who expanded on his words or illustrated them by means of historical examples. In some cases we can see a discussion unfolding as a ruler, by way of testing his would-be general, presents him with increasingly difficult questions to answer. The more of the material one reads, the more one feels that not all of it is meant to be taken seriously; some of it has a playful character as questions, examples and attributions are piled on each other, joining into regular mental battles. To help the student keep the essentials in mind mnemonic devices are often employed, for example 'the five principles', 'the six preservations', 'the nine manoeuvres', and the like.

Finally, the texts in question cannot be understood without bearing in mind the underlying way in which Chinese culture approaches war. War was neither a means in the hands of policy nor, and much less, an end in itself. Instead it was regarded as an evil, albeit one that was sometimes rendered necessary by the imperfection of the world. 'Weapons are instruments of ill omen,' said Sun Tzu, the oldest and most famous general of all, who may or may not have been a historical figure. 'However vast the state, he who takes pleasure in the military will perish,' added Sun Pin, reputed to have lived a century or so after Sun Tzu and to have been the latter's direct descendant. As Wu Tzu told the Marquis of Wei in their first interview, a ruler might not have a liking for military affairs, but not to prepare for war was to fail in his duty: 'When the dead lie stiff and you grieve for them, you have not attained righteousness.' 'War is of vital importance to the state,' said Sun Tzu. Therefore, in the words of Sun Pin, 'military affairs cannot be but investigated'.

Constituting a necessary evil, war was at the same time a temporary departure from 'cosmic harmony', or *Tao*. By definition, *Tao* can only be restored by *Tao*. Hence the war will be won by the side possessing the greatest Virtue, Virtue itself being but another translation of *Tao*. 'You should cultivate your Virtue … and observe the *Tao* of Heaven,' said Ta'i Kung in his Opening Instructions. 'In general, warfare is a question of Heaven, material resources and excellence,' said Ssu-ma. 'Appraise it [i.e. war] in terms of the five fundamental factors,' said Sun Tzu. 'The first of these factors is moral influence … by moral influence I mean that which causes the people to be in harmony with their leaders, so that they will accompany them in life and unto death without fear of mortal peril.' And in the words of Sun Pin, 'Engaging in a battle without

Sun Tzu teaching drill to the concubines of King Ho-lü.

righteousness, no one under Heaven would be able to be solid and strong.'

The military virtue of an army takes the form of strict discipline – or perhaps one should say that, since necessity is not for every private to judge, discipline is the general's way to impose necessity on his troops. A famous story told about Sun Tzu illustrates the point. When Sun Tzu asked the King of Wu, Ho-lü, to employ him as a general, the king in turn asked him if he could fashion an army out of the royal wives and concubines. Sun Tzu said he could, and promptly set about teaching them drill. The women took it as a lark: laughing and joking among themselves, they disobeyed Sun Tzu's instructions. Having explained himself several times over, and seeing himself still disobeyed, he gave orders that the king's two favourite wives be executed. To the king, who tried to intervene, Sun Tzu explained that since he himself was now the commanding general he need not take all the sovereign's orders. After the two had been executed the remainder immediately fell into line and carried out the required exercises. Putting himself at their head, Sun Tzu told the king that they would now be prepared to follow his orders 'through fire and water'.

The need for strict discipline as a basis for all military action is equally evident in the remaining texts. According to Ssu-ma, the perfect army – placed far in the legendary past – is the one that requires neither rewards nor punishments. To make use of rewards but impose no punishments is the height of instruction; to impose punishments but issue no rewards is the height of awesomeness. Finally, employing a mixture of both punishments and rewards – combining sticks with carrots, as modern terminology has it – will end up causing Virtue to decline. Thus the basic idea of *Tao*, which underlines every one of these texts, breaks through once again. Governed by necessity, the best-disciplined army is so good that it requires neither rewards nor punishments. Behaving as if it were a single personality, it will follow its commander of its own accord; although, as the remaining texts make clear, this is an ideal that is rarely if ever attained.

When these matters have been dealt with it is possible to discuss such questions as organization, armaments and supply. According to Wei Liao Tzu, organization was a question of establishing clear regulations so that every soldier would know just what was expected of him. The men (he also speaks of chariots,

OPPOSITE: *First-century AD
statuette of a horseman,
made around the time of
Christ.*

though by the age of the warring states they were obsolete) were to be divided into units five, ten, one hundred, one thousand and ten thousand strong with a single commander in charge of each; in each unit, the strongest and most outstanding soldiers were to be positioned in front. According to Ta'i Kung, the commander-in-chief was to surround himself with the following: a chief of planning; five planning officers; three astrologers; three topographers; nine 'strategists' (what we would call staff officers, 'responsible for discussing divergent views, analysing the probable success or failure of various operations'); four supply officers; and a variety of officers responsible for keeping discipline, gathering intelligence, carrying out engineering jobs, administering medicines and accounting. Command was exercised by using pennants by day, and gongs, drums and whistles by night.

All the texts under consideration are set in a legendary past which is assumed to be both unchanging and far superior to the present. Hence they have relatively little to say about armament; in this respect they differ sharply from our present-day voluminous discussions of the so-called 'Revolution in Military Affairs', which are based on the assumption that the key to warfare is technology. To look at it in another way, in the China of the warring states a revolution in military affairs had already taken place. Cavalry was taking the place of chariots. The use of large formations of infantry was growing; iron weapons had taken the place of bronze, swords that of mere daggers. In his chapter 'Preparation of Strategic Power', Sun Pin gives a succinct account of the evolution of weapons and equipment as well as their use. 'The Yellow Emperor created swords and imagized military formations upon them. Yi created bows and crossbows and imagized strategic power on them. Yu created boats and carts and imagized (tactical)

A model bronze chariot
from c. 210 BC, excavated in
Xi'an, Shaanxi Province in
December 1980. As in the
Middle East during the
same period, chariots were
being replaced by cavalry.

26

changes on them. T'ang and Wu [all these are legendary emperors] made long [i.e. missile] weapons and imagized the strategic imbalance of power on them.' Thus four types of weapons and equipment are listed: the first provides formations with staying power, the second enables users to act from a distance, the third provides mobility (change) and the fourth enables them to dominate the enemy. The art of war consists of combining the four, employing each in correct interaction with the others so as to bring out their advantages and mask their weaknesses. 'If one knows their *Tao* then the army will be successful ...

LEFT: '*Yi created bows and imagized strategic power on them*'; *a kneeling archer from the Terracotta Army.*

LEFT: '*The Yellow Emperor created swords and imagized military formations on them*'; *a scabbard from the third century* BC.

if someone wants to employ them but does not know their *Tao*, the army will lack success.'

Concerning supply, 'money is the sinews of war'. According to Sun Tzu, an army numbering 100,000 men with all its equipment, if led 1,000 li (a Chinese itinerary measure of around 550 metres) into enemy territory, will cost 1,000 gold coins a day to maintain. Included in the calculation are such esoteric items as presents for the commanders' guests and glue for fixing broken chariots; however, the greatest expenditure is that which must cover provisioning. The larger the distance from home, the more ruinous the cost of transport. For that reason, but also because the presence of an army will cause the price of everything to rise, a commander who attempts to support his forces from his own country will ruin the people. It is therefore best to impose the logistic burden on the enemy, a principle that Sun Tzu considers so important that he repeats it twice.

Ta'i Kung, whom I have already quoted, wanted the army to have four officers who would look after the organization of supply. They would be 'responsible for calculating the requirements for food and water; preparing the food stocks and supplies and transporting the provisions along the route; and supplying the five grains so as to ensure that the army will not suffer any hardship or shortage'. Once an army had entered enemy country it was to resort to plunder as a matter of course; conversely, an army operating in a country where there were neither towns and villages to feed the men nor grass to meet the needs of horses and oxen found itself in dire straits. In such a situation, continued Ta'i

Then, as now, money was the sinews of war; Chinese coins dating to the Han dynasty.

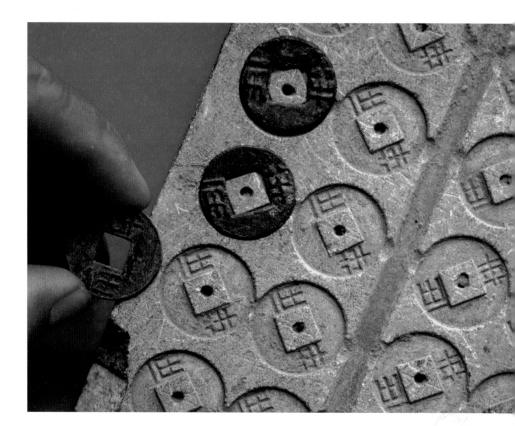

Kung, the commander should 'seek some opportunity to trick the enemy and quickly get away', if necessary by using 'gold and jade' to obtain the necessary intelligence.

Plentiful supplies, everything that is needed by way of arms and equipment, good organization and strict discipline constitute the foundation on which a successful campaign can be built. Provided these are available, the next step is to carry out a survey as to the respective strength of one's own side and that of the enemy. The favour of Heaven apart, four factors are to be considered: first the weather, second the terrain, third command and fourth doctrine. The weather will determine which season is the most favourable for campaigning and how this is to be done. Knowledge of the terrain will enable the general to calculate the size of the forces, the kind of troops needed and what kind of operational plan to adopt. Command refers to the qualities of the opposing general, whereas by doctrine is meant everything that pertains to the organization of the enemy and his supply system. 'There is', sums up Sun Tzu, 'no general who has not heard of these ... matters. Those who master them, win; those who do not, are defeated.'

But how, precisely, is victory to be won? Since violence represents a disturbance of *Tao*, its use should be kept to the indispensable minimum. 'No state has ever benefited from a long war,' said Sun Tzu. 'Those that garner five victories will meet with disaster; those with four victories will be exhausted; those with three victories will become hegemons; those with two victories will be

kings; and those with one victory will become emperors' (Wu Tzu). The best way to settle a dispute, explained Sun Tzu, is by diplomacy as when you negotiate with the enemy and give him presents. Second best is the use of dirty tricks such as assassinating the enemy commander or bribing his officers; those who cannot use dirty tricks engage in manoeuvre. Those who cannot manoeuvre fight a battle, and those who cannot fight a battle lay siege.

In Clausewitz's view, 'the maximum employment of force in no way rules out the use of intelligence'. Not so according to the Chinese commander sages, who, following the fundamental world-view laid down by Lao Tzu, look at the two as opposites and always seek to minimize the first by relying on the second. Force is to be used in carefully measured doses, neither more nor less than is necessary, and in short, sharp bursts. This means that it must be very precisely aimed: 'throw rocks at eggs' is how Sun Tzu puts it in one of those incomparable metaphors that have helped make his work the most famous of all. When you are strong, pretend to be weak so as to tempt the enemy; when you are weak, pretend to be strong so as to deter him. Use speed and

SPIES

The use of spies: 'what enables the wise sovereign and the good general to strike and conquer, and achieve things beyond the reach of ordinary men, is foreknowledge' (Sun Tzu).

secrecy to make out that you are concentrating at one place, then attack at another. If weaker than the enemy, avoid him, harass him and draw him into terrain that is unfavourable for him; if equal to him, wait patiently until he commits an error, as in chess. Confuse him and keep him ignorant of your designs by offering bait, mounting feints and/or spreading disinformation as appropriate. Finally, when you have the enemy where you want him – in other words, just when he feels secure – fall on him like a thunderbolt.

Thus the strongest, most successful action is at the same time the most economic one. To achieve this ideal, two things are needed. The first is extreme flexibility which will enable one to take advantage of fleeting opportunities: said Sun Tzu, 'an army is like water which adapts itself to the configuration of the ground'. Plans must have many branches and be so arranged that alternative ones can be put into operation without undue disruption. Forces earmarked for one mission must be capable of switching to another, if necessary at a moment's notice and with neither commanders nor troops missing a heartbeat. In all this there can be no fixed routine, no unalterable *modus operandi*, but only as many stratagems as there are enemies and circumstances.

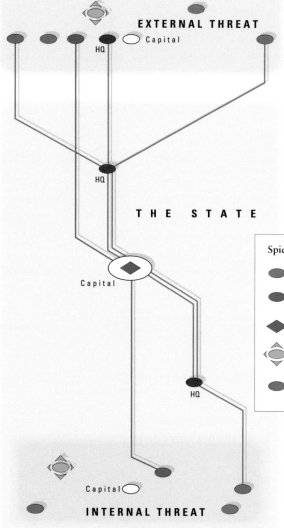

The second requirement is, of course, intelligence. Sun Tzu distinguishes between five different types of spies: local spies, internal spies, turned spies, dead spies and the living spy. Local spies are simply travellers and residents of the theatre of war who are examined concerning the terrain, its resources and whatever they may know of the enemy. Internal spies are people who hold positions inside the enemy's forces. Turned spies are double agents, i.e. the enemy's spies who have been forced or persuaded to work for one's own side. Dead (expendable) spies are sent out into the enemy camp for the purpose of spreading disinformation. Finally, living spies consist of one's own agents who are expected to return and deliver reports. The entire question of espionage requires 'the wisdom of a sage' both when it comes to perceiving the truth of incoming reports and in

'Handling spies requires the wisdom of a sage'; an eighteenth-century painting of Confucius (on the right).

handling those valuable but difficult creatures, the spies themselves. 'There are no areas in which one does not employ spies.'

Correctly and systematically employed, espionage will endow the commander with a thorough understanding of the enemy, including, above all, his strengths and weaknesses. The art of war demands that the former be avoided and the latter exploited; in other words, that the enemy's qualities be made to mesh, or synchronize, with one's own. Thus knowing oneself is no less, and may be more, of a requirement than understanding the enemy. According to Ta'i Kung, '"Know them and know yourself" is the great essence of military strategy. Contemporary generals, even if they do not know the enemy, ought to be able to know themselves, so how could they lose the advantage?' Said Sun Tzu: 'Know the enemy and know yourself; in a hundred battles you will never be in peril. When you are ignorant of the enemy but know yourself, your chances of winning or losing are equal. If ignorant both of your enemy and of yourself, you are certain in every battle to be in peril.' To which the commentator Li Chu'an added: 'Such people are called "mad bandits". What can they expect if not defeat?'

In spite of their antiquarian bent, which leads to the discussion of out-of-date weapons and sometimes gives the whole a quaint air, for sheer sophistication Chinese military writings have never been equalled. In them high seriousness alternates with play, pungent sayings with relaxed discussion, abstract analysis with an abundance of concrete examples taken from the annals of the warring states and more often than not associated with the names of famous generals; yet seldom do they descend to the kind of technical trivia which, as we shall presently see, mark much of classical Western military thought. An underlying humanity pervades all: '[Virtue is] sparing the people from death, eliminating the hardships of the people, relieving the misfortunes of the people, and sustaining the people in their extremities' (Ta'i Kung). This is combined with a readiness to ignore personal considerations concerning love and hate, take the most drastic measures (including such as we should consider underhand or immoral), and inflict the harshest punishments; all as may be dictated by necessity which knows no bounds. Above all, no clear line is drawn between military affairs and the rest of life. On the contrary, it is a question of achieving *Tao* in the military field also.

As in the rest of life, the best way to achieve *Tao* is not to depart from it in the first place. To paraphrase, the best war is that which is never fought. The second best is that which is avoided, the third that which is won without bloodshed, the fourth that which involves heavy loss of life, and the fifth that which has to be repeated time after time. As in Plato's *Republic*, which was written at approximately the same time and where the state is made to stand as a metaphor for the human soul, all five ways of behaviour apply not just to the ruler but to the private individual too. The first marks the way of the commander-in-chief who is also a sage; the last, that of the man who is both brutal and stupid. Yet

'Usefulness arises from
whatever is not'; Lao Tzu
('the Old Master') leaving
his home to save the world,
riding on a bull.

praiseworthy as an inclination towards peace may be, on no account should it lead to a neglect of military affairs: 'Those who forget warfare will inevitably be endangered' (Ta'i Kung). Perhaps it is impossible to do better than to sum up in the words of Lao Tzu, 'the Old Master'. While not a military expert, he was the father of *Tao*-ism and thus stands at the root of every one of the texts we have discussed:

> Once grasp the great form without a form
> and you will roam where you will
> with no evil to fear,
> calm, peaceful, at ease.
> The hub of the wheel runs upon the axle.
> In a jar, it is the hole that holds water.
> So advantage is had
> from whatever there is;
> but usefulness rises
> from whatever is not.

CHAPTER TWO

From Antiquity to the Middle Ages

A RATHER FANCIFUL *siege tower as shown in*
a German edition of Vegetius, 1529.

FROM ANTIQUITY TO THE MIDDLE AGES

W HEN IT COMES TO the writing of military history, Classical antiquity has never been surpassed. Thucydides and Sallust and Caesar and Josephus: in the entire record of mankind one looks in vain for authors better capable of describing the goals of commanders, the activities of armies, the motivations of troops, the possibilities and limitations of weapons and the sufferings of civilians. Not quite on the same level, but still very impressive, are the works of Herodotus, Xenophon, Polybios and Livy (although from the Renaissance to the Enlightenment it was usually the last-named who was regarded as the greatest historian of all). Both Herodotus and Livy wrote patriotic history and are perhaps a trifle too inclined towards the legendary, the supernatural and the moralistic to suit our supposedly 'scientific' taste. Xenophon, though a competent commander and a superb journalist, does not have psychological depth. Polybios represents the point of view of the Hellenistic magistrate and diplomat. As such he certainly knew his business but tended to be dry and technical.

Against this grand tradition *in historicis*, it is remarkable that ancient

LEFT: *Josephus Flavius: a nineteenth-century engraving showing him in Turkish dress.*

RIGHT: A *Roman copy of a fourth-century Greek bust of Herodotus, known as the 'father of history'.*

military theory does not attain nearly the same level of excellence. Certainly this is not due to the absence of great generals; who in the whole of history can equal an Alexander, a Hannibal, a Scipio or a Caesar? Yet with the exception of the last-named in his *commentarii*, which are exactly what they claim to be, none of them has left us a first-hand record of his experiences, much less tried to develop them into a systematic treatise on the art of war. Such treatises as do exist, and

*During the Renaissance,
Livy was considered the
greatest of all ancient
historians. This illustration
shows a 1523 German
edition of his work.*

there are quite a few, were written by decidedly second-rate figures. Like their
Chinese counterparts most, though probably not all, had some personal
experience of war. Unlike their Chinese counterparts none seems to have
commanded at the highest level, let alone acquired fame as a great general.

Disregarding Xenophon, whose *Cyropaedia* constitutes not so much military
analysis as a semi-imaginary tale concerning the ways of a successful prince, the

Hannibal's elephants in battle; a 1925 painting by André Bauchant.

earliest writer whose work is extant is Aeneas the Tactician in the fourth century BC. The last from the ancient world is Vegetius, who must have written at the very end of the fourth century AD. Judging by the examples which he does and does not adduce, Aeneas wrote before either Philip or Alexander the Great appeared on the scene and transformed Greek warfare. By contrast, Vegetius belongs to the period when the Roman Empire was being metamorphosed into the Byzantine one. Perhaps the fact that they are separated by a gap of almost seven centuries explains why these writers, in contrast with their Chinese opposite numbers, neither possess a common ideology nor adhere to a single world-view.

Starting then with Aeneas, one may note that he was the author of a number of treatises on the art of war all but one of which has been lost. The one which survives deals with a single, highly technical question, namely how to defend a besieged city against attack. Chapter 1 deals with the disposition of troops and the preparation of positions. Chapter 2 explains how morale is to be maintained and attempts at treachery and revolution thwarted, an extremely important question in Greek city states which, at the time when Aeneas wrote, were often threatened by factional strife even as the enemy was at the gates. Chapter 3 explains how sudden raids ought to be foiled. Chapter 4 deals with keeping the enemy away from the walls, chapter 5 with methods for guarding the walls, and chapter 6 with how to meet actual assaults upon the walls and repulse them. All this is done in a competent enough way and often in considerable detail: for example, there are so and so many methods by which a city's gates can be unlocked and which, accordingly, ought to be guarded against by those who bear the responsibility. Similarly, the passwords with which patrols are issued ought to be carefully selected for memorability and recognizability. Sentries should not be allowed to leave their posts before their replacements have arrived. When sawing through the bolt of a gate, pour on oil so as to proceed faster and make less noise, and so forth down to the suggestion that, to make a few soldiers appear like many, they should be made to march in lines abreast with each successive rank carrying their spears on alternate shoulders.

In military science as in so many others, attention to detail is absolutely vital and cannot be dispensed with. In military science as in so many others, attention to detail is not enough and does not automatically translate into genius. Some of the devices which Aeneas suggests – particularly those which deal with encoding methods – appear naïve; others, such as a kind of optical telegraph for the transmission of messages, were impractical and already subjected to criticism in ancient times. But on the whole his is a useful collection of rules and devices which any competent person appointed to defend a town ought to have at his fingertips. Had this author selected a motto, no doubt it would have been 'for want of a nail a city was lost'.

As far as can be reconstructed, Aeneas' remaining writings dealt with 'military preparations', 'war finance', 'encampments', 'plots', 'naval tactics', 'historical illustrations' and 'siege warfare'. Supposing these to have been of a similar character to the one which still exists, then a person who had mastered them all ought to have had at his disposal a vast depository of admittedly somewhat pedestrian military knowledge. It would have come in handy in almost any situation, provided of course sufficient time was available to consult the many volumes in which it was contained. It would not have been of any help at all in the planning of war at the highest level.

No such praise may be bestowed on our next text, Asclepiodotus' *Outline of Tactics*. As far as can be determined Asclepiodotus, who flourished around the middle of the first century BC, was a student of the great Stoic philosopher Poseidonius. Unlike Aeneas he was not a military man, and indeed the treatise itself may have been written merely as an exercise in rhetoric. At the time the *Tactics* was written its main subject, i.e. the Greek phalanx, was long out of date and the Roman legion, as used for example by Pompey and Julius Caesar, was approaching its zenith. Yet nothing in Asclepiodotus' work indicates that he was living in an age of military genius; instead the book takes the original Greek meaning of 'tactics', i.e. 'order', literally. It contains an extremely pedantic discussion of the distances to be kept between the men in the phalanx, the length of their spears, the width of their shields, the titles of the leaders of various sub-formations and how to make the men turn right or left without falling into disorder. The treatise ends in a long list of orders such as: 'Stand by to take arms!' (*parastethi epi ta hopla*, to give the reader who is not a classicist an idea of what it sounded like), 'Silence in the ranks!' and 'Attention! Baggage-men fall out! Take up arms! Shoulder arms!' It is the Greek drill-master whose voice we hear.

The phalanx apart, Asclepiodotus also includes brief discussions of light infantry (peltasts), cavalry, chariots and elephants. However, they are even less inspiring than the rest and indeed one gets the impression that, by the time he reaches the last two, the author himself, aware that they are hopelessly out of date, can scarcely suppress a yawn. The entire work bears an abstract character, failing as it does to adduce a single example drawn from actual military life; nor does it even attempt to discuss the way in which the various kinds of troops ought to interact with each other and the enemy, i.e. tactics as we would understand the term. Still, as one modern author has commented, it is useful to know that there existed a Macedonian, a Laconian and a Cretan counter-march and that the last of these was also known as the Persian. Not to forget the earth-shaking fact that the leader of a single elephant was known as an animal-commander (*zoarchos*) and of two, as a beast-commander (*therarchos*).

Like Asclepiodotus, who wrote about one hundred years earlier, Onasander was primarily a student of philosophy. His work, entitled *O Strategos* (The General), may also have been intended as an exercise in rhetoric, but if so it must be admitted that it is considerably less technical than that of his predecessor. Having dedicated his book 'to the Romans, and especially to those of the Romans who have attained senatorial dignity and who through the wisdom of Augustus Caesar [Nero is meant] have been raised to the power of consul or general', he proposes to discuss everything that pertains to the good commander. First things first: the post of commander must be taken by one who is 'temperate, self-restrained, vigilant, frugal, hardened to labour, alert, free from avarice, neither too young nor too old, indeed a father of children if possible, a ready speaker and a man with a good reputation'. The bulk of Onasander's first chapter consists of a very sensible explanation as to why each quality is needed.

The rest of the treatise is equally balanced and unexciting. Chapters 2 and 3 (each chapter is no more than a page or so long) describe the character which the subordinate officers must have as well as the need for the commander to have an

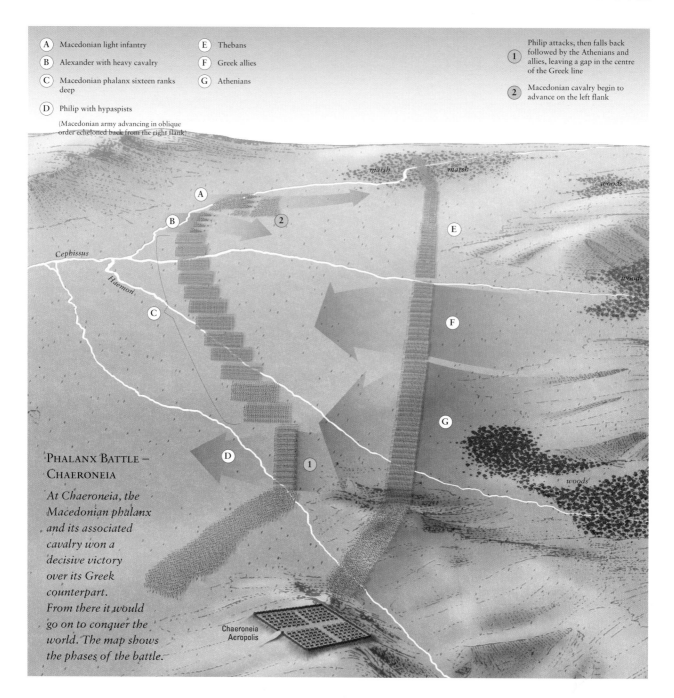

(A) Macedonian light infantry

(B) Alexander with heavy cavalry

(C) Macedonian phalanx sixteen ranks deep

(D) Philip with hypaspists

(Macedonian army advancing in oblique order echeloned back from the right flank)

(E) Thebans

(F) Greek allies

(G) Athenians

(1) Philip attacks, then falls back followed by the Athenians and allies, leaving a gap in the centre of the Greek line

(2) Macedonian cavalry begin to advance on the left flank

PHALANX BATTLE – CHAERONEIA

At Chaeroneia, the Macedonian phalanx and its associated cavalry won a decisive victory over its Greek counterpart. From there it would go on to conquer the world. The map shows the phases of the battle.

Chaeroneia Acropolis

Cephissus

Haemon

marsh

marsh

woods

woods

woods

A Macedonian phalanx

The Macedonian phalanx, up to sixteen men deep as against the Greek eight to twelve, offered more offensive power but was more vulnerable from the flanks. Its main armament was the long pike that was intended for forward motion only.

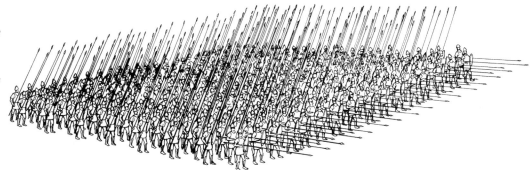

3 Alexander advances through a gap in the Greek line and cuts off the Theban right flank

4 Philip resumes his advance against the Athenians

5 The Athenians, on seeing their right flank trapped by Philip's advance, give way and retreat, followed by Macedonian phalanx who maintain discipline and formation

The Battle of Chaeroneia

Philip of Macedon, fielding just over 30,000 men, destroyed an Athenian–Theban allied army of over 50,000. The backbone of Philip's army was its disciplined infantry organized in the Macedonian version of the Greek phalanx. Constant training enabled the Macedonians to perform a variety of movements beyond the capabilities of their enemies.

Cephissus

Haemon

marsh

marsh

woods

woods

woods

Chaeroneia Acropolis

advisory council of some sort. Chapters 4 and 5 deal with the need to have a reasonable, real not unjust, cause for war, as well as the importance of listening to soothsayers and omens. Chapters 6 and 7 deal with the maintenance of military formations, and here too Onasander's advice is sensible enough. Order should be maintained at all times. Depending on the country in question, i.e. whether it is wide open or narrow, formations should be either broad or deep. The former is better suited for fighting, the latter for marching; other things being equal, some compromise between them should be found. Vulnerable elements of the army, such as its medical equipment, pack animals and baggage, should be placed either in the centre of the column or, in case the latter comes under attack, on the side that is farthest away from the enemy. Allied country is not to be plundered and the question of supply is to be attended to.

Like Asclepiodotus, Onasander does not provide any examples to illustrate or clarify his meaning (though it must be admitted that his meaning is almost always

perfectly clear). Unlike Asclepiodotus (or Aeneas), only rarely does his advice degenerate into trivia. The discussion of the way the different arms ought to be arrayed and co-operate with each other points to real insight on his part, albeit that unfortunately the force he has in mind is not the Roman legion of his day but the long-obsolete phalanx. Various tactics, such as the feigned retreat, the need to hold some troops in reserve so as to assist formations that have become exhausted and the effectiveness of sudden attacks directed against the enemy's flank and rear, are discussed. All this is done in a sensible if curiously bloodless manner, and again without any illustrations or examples.

Thus far the arrangement of the material is reasonable and orderly. From chapter 23 onwards it degenerates, however, losing coherence as the author jumps from one subject to the next without really bothering to maintain any particular order. While scarcely sensational, much of the advice proffered continues to be quite sensible: for example, the need for a general to make the troops look after

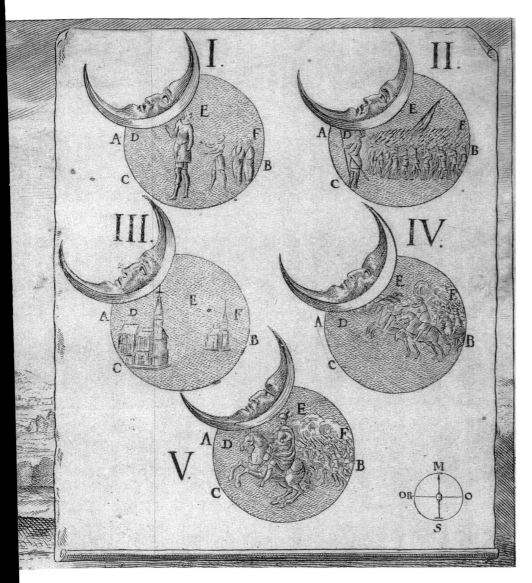

This illustration shows a campaign planned in accordance with the phases of an eclipse. Military textbooks written at any time between 400 BC and AD 1700 often contain material on the need to consult soothsayers and astrologers as to whether an action is auspicious or not. The illustration is from a seventeenth-century work on the wars between the Austrian Empire and the Ottomans.

One of the aqueducts leading to Rome, the Claudian aqueduct, for which Frontinus was responsible.

their equipment or to avoid fighting in person; victorious troops should be justly rewarded, defeated ones encouraged; cities that have surrendered fairly treated, the dead buried and the gods always honoured by performing the appropriate rites. In sum, a 'good man' who attends to all these 'will not only be a brave defender of his fatherland and a competent leader of an army but also, for the permanent protection of his own reputation, will be a sagacious strategist'.

In our own day the works of Aeneas, Asclepiodotus and Onasander have long been dead – and understandably so, given the dry, schematic and sometimes pettifogging way in which they approach their subjects. Not so during the period from about 1450 to 1700 when 'the ancients' were revived by humanist scholarship and enjoyed high esteem. Onasander's work in particular was described as 'the most learned, concise and valuable [treatise] to be found upon the art of war' (Francis Guilliman, 1583); but this is even more true of the next two authors we must consider, Frontinus and Vegetius. Both of them were not 'dead' at all, but reissued and translated and considered to be of immediate practical use to commanders of the Renaissance and beyond.

Sextus Julius Frontinus was a Roman official whose career spanned the last quarter of the first century AD and who accumulated considerable experience, both military – he fought the tribes in what is now Wales – and as a civilian in his capacity as supervisor of the Rome's aqueducts. His main work on the art of war has been lost; what remains is the *Strategemata*, best translated as 'tricks of the

trade' and apparently meant to serve as a companion to the theoretical treatise. It consists of four books of which the last one was written by another person. Unlike so many others it has nothing to say about raising troops, formations, discipline, etc.; instead it is divided into fifty chapters with titles such as 'Distracting the Attention of the Enemy', 'By What Means the Enemy May be Reduced to Want', 'On Terrorizing the Besieged' and 'On the Effect of Discipline'. Each chapter contains a list of devices used by past commanders in the realization of their plans. For example, 'whenever Alexander of Macedon had a strong army he chose the sort of warfare in which he could fight in open battle'. An ambassador of Scipio Africanus who was conducting a parley once deliberately had a horse run wild in the enemy's camp, presenting his men with an opportunity to chase it around and thus observe more than they should have. The Carthaginians, lacking material for cordage, used their women's hair to equip their fleet. Caesar once spurred his soldiers to battle by showering such praise on his Tenth Legion that the rest became envious and wanted to emulate it.

Since Frontinus makes no attempt to link the various

Alexander always led from the front and was wounded many times. This amphora shows him with lance in hand, charging Emperor Darius in his four-horse chariot.

devices with each other, as an exercise in monotony his work has seldom been equalled. Yet it must be conceded that, so long as the technical limitations of his age are borne in mind, many of his suggestions were practical. A commander capable of employing only a small fraction of them would be considered highly inventive, which presumably explains why he was quite popular in antiquity and remained so throughout the Middle Ages and beyond. When the great scholar Jean Gerson (1363–1429) drew up a list of works which ought to be in the library

The Roman statesman and general Cato as he appears on a playing card dating to the French Revolution. At that time his supposed qualities of austerity and patriotism were much in vogue.

of the French Dauphin he included Frontinus. Machiavelli, who though a far greater writer also possessed a practical mind not so very different from Frontinus' own, considered him indispensable. He continued to be read, and quoted, by commanders down to the third quarter of the eighteenth century.

Writing some three centuries after Frontinus, Flavius Renatus Vegetius, with his *Epitoma Rei Militaris* (A Summary of Military Matters), stands in a class all of his own. Apparently Vegetius, who was not a soldier but an administrator in

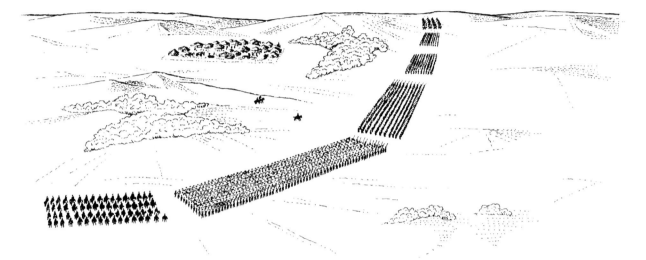

the Imperial service, produced the work on behalf of a Roman emperor by the name of Valentian – we do not know which one of two possible candidates he had in mind – who, faced with the much weakened state of the Empire, wanted to know how the 'ancient' Romans had gone about their business so successfully. Consequently he does not deal with the army of his own day but with an idealized version of previous ones. Among the sources which he mentions are Cato, Sallust and Frontinus, and the military ordinances of Augustus, Trajan and Hadrian. Thus it is likely that the military organization which Vegetius describes never existed at any single time and place. Still, it is a tribute to his work that he succeeds in bringing it to life and presenting us with a remarkably coherent whole.

Of the four parts, the first one discusses recruits, their selection ('fishermen, fowlers, confectioners, weavers, and all those who appear to have been engaged in occupations appropriate to women should not, in my opinion, be allowed near the barracks') and their training in marching, the use of arms and the various formations which are used in battle. Part 2 gives the best account of the legion's organization which we have or are likely to have, including its organization and the sub-units of which it consists, the officers, the promotion system, the auxiliary services, its troop of horse, and the way in which it ought to be drawn up for battle. Part 3 deals with the various tactical methods which were used by the legion, part 4 (which seems to have been tagged on by another writer) with fortifications and naval warfare. Yet precisely because he does not focus on any

THE ADVANCE

An army advancing according to the rules set down in the Strategikon, *a treatise produced by the Byzantine Empire and attributed to the Emperor Maurice.*

particular period, Vegetius' work is as much prescriptive as it is descriptive. From beginning to end the importance of thorough training, strong discipline, hard work (as in building a fortified camp each night) and sound planning are emphasized; in particular, part 3 ends with a long list of dos and don'ts, such as 'it is better to have several bodies of reserves than to extend your front too much' and 'troops are not to be led into battle unless they are confident of success'. *Epitoma*'s succinct style, plus the fact that it was dedicated to an emperor and thus contained a direct link with the prestige of Imperial Rome, and the many useful suggestions it contains in regard to fortification in particular, explain why, for over a thousand years after it was written, it remained the most popular of any military handbook – in 1770 one Austrian field marshal, the Prince de Ligne, went so far as to claim that 'Vegetius had been inspired by God'. He was considered the greatest writer of all, even in the Middle Ages when the core of armies consisted of cavalry rather than the infantry of which he wrote.

Both the *Strategemata* and the *Epitoma* were written in Latin, which is another reason why they were so popular during the Middle Ages in Europe. Not so, of course, the military treatises produced by the Byzantine Empire. The best-known one, the *Strategikon*, is attributed to the Emperor Maurice (reigned 582–602) but in fact was composed in his name by others. Written not long after the great campaigns of Belisarius and Narses, it represents Byzantine military practice at its zenith. Part 1, comprising the introduction, describes the training, equipment and discipline of the *tagma*, a cavalry formation which had taken the place of the infantry legion. (Reflecting the much-diminished importance of infantry in Byzantine times, it is dealt with only in part 12 along with mixed formations, camps and hunting.) Parts 2 and 3 deal with the way in which the *tagma* ought to be prepared and positioned for battle. Part 4 advises the commander on how to deal with ambushes and set them up; part 5 discusses the way baggage trains are to be arrayed and part 6 various tactics and drills to be used when confronting the enemy. The subject of part 7 is 'generalship' (*strategia*). Far from dealing with matters of supreme import pertaining to the overall conduct of the campaign, however, it is subtitled 'the points which the general must consider'. These include blessing the flags, organizing the squads, gathering enemy intelligence, making speeches to encourage the troops, interrogating prisoners, punishing offenders, watering the horses and making sure that the men carry rations in their saddlebags.

A general who has followed the *Strategikon*'s instructions up to this point ought to have his army ready and drawn up for battle. Accordingly, part 8 deals with 'points to be observed on the day of battle', such as the need for the general not to overburden himself and to conceal his intentions for as long as possible. Part 9 deals with methods for launching surprise attacks, and part 10 with offensive and defensive siege-operations including 'building a border fortress by stealth and without open battle'. Obviously produced by a group of experts, all this material makes very good sense. And indeed traces of its influence on

ca oster donte· les nouns de dusse non pas soule
ment en greu· mes ensement en latin· ad il auant
tuche·

De tuz ces venz souentesez en grāt tempestes soler
env· ii· ou treil soffler ensemble· par sofflemet
de ces venz· les mers lu sunt paisibles par lor voil·
e deboneires par les undes estriuanz se desuient· par
sofflement de ceus por nature detent ou des luis des
tempestes est rendu clarte· car en le seoind soffle

Ci commence le V.e liure charlemame premiere
ment de la trahison que guenelon pourchata
uis que charlemame le tres
puissant ? tresrenome empeu
eut conquise toute la terre
despaigne ? galice ? soubz
mise a la foy crestiene en lo
neur de dieu ? de monseigneur saint iacques
Il retourna en france ? fist ses ostz herbergier
delez la bonne cite de pampeline Sn cellui
temps demouroient en la cite de sarragote deux
roys sarrazins le roy marsillon ? son frere bi

questions such as castrametation (the making of camps) are said to be discernible in the conduct of actual campaigns such as the one against the Arabs in AD 636.

Even more interesting, both to the historian and probably also to the contemporary commander, is part 11, which provides brief anthropological analyses of the principal enemies facing the Empire, their weaknesses and their strengths, and suggests ways for dealing with each one. For example, 'the Persian nation is wicked, dissembling and servile, but at the same time patriotic and obedient'. Seldom bothering to look after their flanks, 'they are vulnerable to attacks and encirclements from an outflanking position against the flanks and rear of their formations' and should, if possible, be engaged on 'open, smooth, and level terrain ... without any swamps, ditches or brush which could break up the [Byzantine] formation'. By contrast, 'the light-haired races place great value on freedom. They are bold and undaunted in battle; daring and impetuous as they are, they consider any timidity and even a short retreat as a disgrace'. However, 'they are hurt by suffering and fatigue ... [as well as] heat, cold, rain, lack of provisions (especially of wine) and postponement of battle'. Therefore, 'in warring against them one must avoid engaging in pitched battles, especially in the early stages, but make use of well-planned ambushes, sneak attacks and stratagems'.

Compared with the *Strategikon*, a masterpiece of sorts, the other Byzantine works on military art which have come down to us – all that remains of a vast literature – are less comprehensive and less informative. The earliest is an anonymous sixth-century treatise whose main subjects are siege warfare on the one hand and the operations of the cavalry phalanx on the other. Then we have the *Tacticon*, an essay on military organization and battle arrays attributed to Emperor Leo the Wise (866–912); though usually mentioned in the same breath as the *Strategikon*, it is in fact much less interesting and less original, being largely an abbreviation of its predecessor as well as containing entire passages lifted straight out of Onasander. The list is completed by two late ninth-century essays, one on skirmishing said to have been the work of Emperor Nicephorus, and an anonymous one on campaign organization. All these volumes reflect the workings of a highly sophisticated, articulated armed force with numerous subdivisions and an emphasis on combined arms. As might perhaps be expected from the 'Byzantines', all of them also display a strong penchant for secrecy, flexibility, cunning and guile in order to achieve victory. In this respect they resemble the Chinese classics; however, since war is regarded purely as an instrument in the hands of the emperor, the underlying humanitarianism which makes the Chinese works so attractive is entirely absent.

During the time when the Byzantine Empire flourished, much of Western Europe had been overrun by barbarian tribes. Their preferred form of military literature, if that is the term, consisted of the *chansons de geste*, narrative songs in which the (usually legendary) exploits of (usually legendary) heroes were celebrated. *La Chanson de Roland* (from the early twelfth century) is the most famous composition of all, but there are many others of varying literary quality. Even later, when the higher classes at any rate ceased being illiterate, the Latin West, in spite of its marked warlike qualities, did not have either professional soldiers or standing armies and, possibly as a result, produced remarkably little by way of military textbooks. Since Byzantine works only became available after the humanist revival, the most popular treatises by far were those of Frontinus and Vegetius, as already noted; the latter in particular graced many a princely

This fourteenth-century French illustration shows King Richard the Lionheart embarking on the Third Crusade in 1190.

library of which we are informed, including that of Richard the Lionheart. These two were supplemented by a number of others whose subject was not so much military theory and practice as the art of 'chivalry' and the rules of war. An outstanding specimen is Honoré Bonet, whose *L'Arbre des batailles* (The Tree of Battles) was written around 1400. A monk and a doctor of law, Bonet's professed goal was to help mitigate the evils of war – this was the Hundred Years War – which, as a native of Provence, he could see all around him.

Nineteenth-century painters prided themselves on the historical accuracy of their work. In this painting, produced in 1830, Eugène Delacroix shows King John II of France being captured in the battle of Poitiers, 1356, during the Hundred Years War.

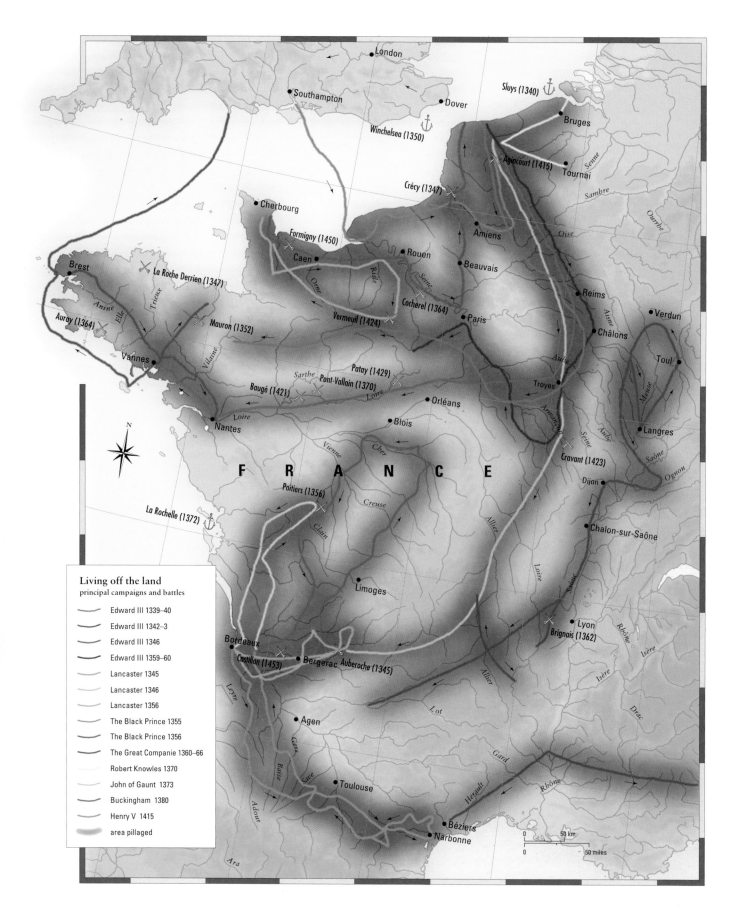

London

Southampton
Dover

Sluys (1340) ⚓

Bruges

Winchelsea (1350) ⚓

Agincourt (1415)
Tournai
Senne

Crécy (1347)

Sambre

Ourthe

Cherbourg

Formigny (1450)

Caen

Rouen

Amiens

Oise

Beauvais

Risle

Brest

La Roche Derrien (1347)

Anine

Elle

Trieux

Cocherel (1364)

Seine

Orne

Vermeuil (1424)

Reims

Paris

Verdun

Châlons

Auray (1364)

Mauron (1352)

Vilaine

Vannes

Sarthe

Patay (1429)

Pont-Vallain (1370)

Baugé (1421)

Loire

Troyes

Toul

Meuse

Aube

Aisne

Armançon

Saône

Nantes

Loire

Orléans

Blois

Langres

Vienne

Cher

Cravant (1423)

Ognon

F R A N C E

Poitiers (1356)

Creuse

Dijon

Chalon-sur-Saône

La Rochelle (1372) ⚓

Clain

Limoges

Allier

Loire

Rhône

Lyon

Brignais (1362)

Isère

Living off the land
principal campaigns and battles

Bordeaux

Castillon (1453)

Bergerac Auberoche (1345)

Allier

Isère

Drac

Edward III 1339–40
Edward III 1342–3
Edward III 1346
Edward III 1359–60
Lancaster 1345
Lancaster 1346
Lancaster 1356
The Black Prince 1355
The Black Prince 1356
The Great Companie 1360–66
Robert Knowles 1370
John of Gaunt 1373
Buckingham 1380
Henry V 1415
area pillaged

Leyre

Agen

Lot

Gard

Gers

Baïse

Save

Toulouse

Hérault

Rhône

Adour

Béziers

Narbonne

0   50 km

0   50 miles

Ara

In the introduction he defines war as 'a discord or conflict that has arisen on account of certain things displeasing to the human will, to the end that such conflict should be turned into agreement and reason'. Next, to determine 'whence came jurisdiction' (i.e. the origins of the laws which he cites), he gives a brief historical account of 'the four great kingdoms of the past', namely Babylon, Persia, Alexander's and Rome. The core of the book, however, consists of several hundred questions and answers concerning the things that are and are not permitted: 'If a soldier has accepted wages for a year, may he put another man in his place during that period?', 'Whether it is lawful to give battle on a feast day',

The recapture of Paris from the English during the Hundred Years War, 1396, by the French painter Jean Berthélemy, dated late eighteenth century.

OPPOSITE: *Christine de Pisan, who was perhaps the first woman writer in history to support herself by her work, also authored a treatise on chivalry. Here she is shown presenting a book to King Charles V of France.*

Towards the end of the Hundred Years War, a military camp may have looked like this.

'Whether the holder of a safe-conduct may take with him a man of higher estate than himself', 'Whether clerics should pay taillages or impositions levied for the purposes of a war' (they should not), 'If a baron is a vassal of two lords who are at war with each other, which should he help?' and 'Whether an English student dwelling in Paris for purposes of study could be imprisoned' (this, remember, is a time of war between France and England).

To those who would understand the mentality of war in the Middle Ages Bonet's work, like that of his self-professed disciple Christine de Pisan, is invaluable. Neither they nor the various chronicles constitute military theory, however, and they are mentioned here only by way of an indication of the kinds of writing which the period in question produced. Summing up the present chapter, one may perhaps conclude that such theory did not constitute a strong point either of the Latin Middle Ages or of the ancient world. Ignoring the differences that existed between their own feudal system and the Roman Imperial one, medieval people were content with a small number of Roman texts which had been handed down and of which they made use as best they could. The ancient world saw the writing of much superb military history; however, judging

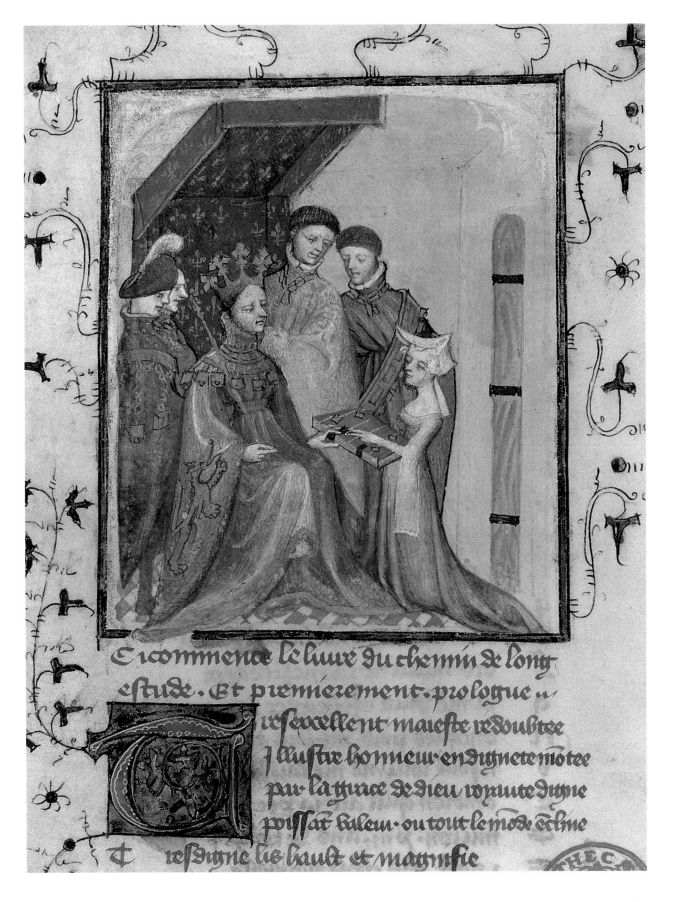

Et commence le liure du chemin de long
estuse. Et premierement. prologue ..
                    tres excellent maieste redoubtee
                    Illustre honneur en dignete motee
                    par la grace de dieu roynie digne
                    puissat baleur. ou tout le mode enclme
            t redigne les hault et magnifie

by what remains, the theoretical treatises which it produced tended to be no more than sensible at best and pedestrian at worst. As to the Byzantine texts, they formed a world apart. Though obviously written for the most part by persons who knew what they were talking about, they exercised little influence outside a small circle of Imperial generals who may have wanted to know such things as (quoting the one on campaign organization) 'how to avoid confusion inside the camp'. These generals may have carried them about and used them as the situation demanded.

What is more, and as their arrangement suggests, even the best of the works discussed in the present chapter are little more than handbooks. They make suggestions and proffer advice which may be appropriate to this occasion or

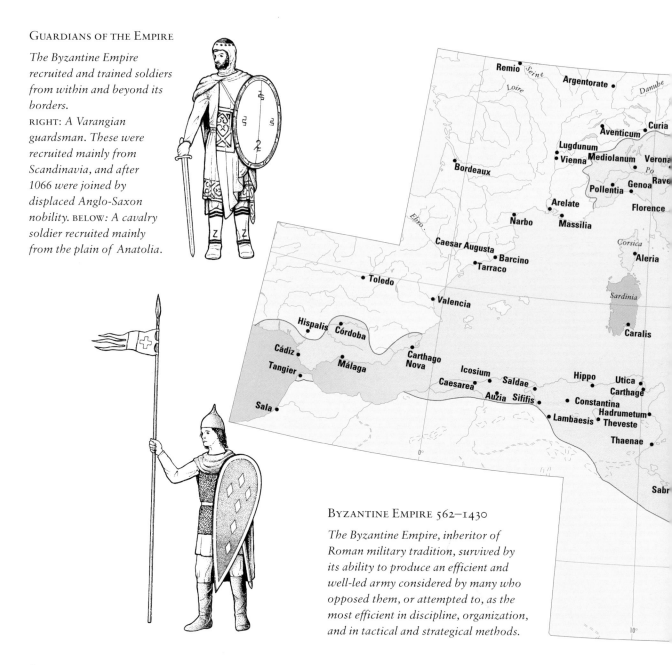

Guardians of the Empire

The Byzantine Empire recruited and trained soldiers from within and beyond its borders.
RIGHT: *A Varangian guardsman. These were recruited mainly from Scandinavia, and after 1066 were joined by displaced Anglo-Saxon nobility.* BELOW: *A cavalry soldier recruited mainly from the plain of Anatolia.*

Byzantine Empire 562–1430

The Byzantine Empire, inheritor of Roman military tradition, survived by its ability to produce an efficient and well-led army considered by many who opposed them, or attempted to, as the most efficient in discipline, organization, and in tactical and strategical methods.

that; taking the formations and armament of their own day more or less for granted, however, they seldom rise above the specifics of time and place. From time to time they go lower still, delving into such questions as the use of heated vinegar for splitting rocks and how to train archers to fire accurately. The fact that some of them were still in use until 1700 and beyond shows how indebted early modern Europe felt itself to be to the ancient world – or, conversely, how slow the evolution of warfare was. Unlike the Chinese classics they do not provide a coherent philosophy of war. In the West, the only writer who met that demand was Clausewitz. Before we can turn to an examination of his work, however, it is necessary to fill in the gap between about 1500 and the end of the Seven Years War.

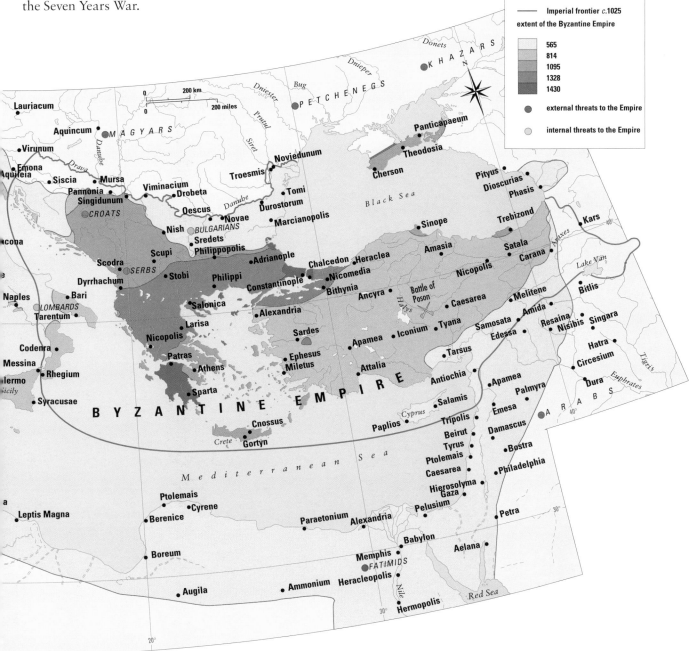

Byzantine Empire
562–1430

—— Imperial frontier *c.*1025

extent of the Byzantine Empire

- 565
- 814
- 1095
- 1328
- 1430

● external threats to the Empire

○ internal threats to the Empire

CHAPTER THREE

———— ❖ ❖◗◯◖❖ ❖ ————

FROM 1500 TO 1763

KING FREDERICK II OF PRUSSIA was one of history's greatest commanders as well as the author of numerous works on the art of war.

FROM 1500 TO 1763

Niccolò Machiavelli's place among the great political scientists of history is secure, and deservedly so. No one who has compared *Il Principe* (The Prince) to, say, Erasmus' *Institutes Principis Christiani* (Ways of a Christian Prince: I prefer this translation to the usual 'Education of a Christian Prince') can but note the immense gap between them: though separated by no more than two

Niccolò Machiavelli, author of L'Arte della Guerra, *was presented as the embodiment of falsehood; painting by Santi di Tito from the second half of the sixteenth century.*

or three years, the latter is a treatise on morals, the former on power. Machiavelli's insights into the nature of power have rarely been equalled, never surpassed. They remain as fresh today as they were when he put them down in 1512–13.

In spite of the attempts made by modern historians to include Machiavelli among the 'makers of modern strategy', *L'Arte della Guerra* (The Art of War) is not a first-class treatise on the subject. Written in 1520–21, the work is cast in the form of a conversation which takes place in a Florentine garden. The chief

character is Fabrizio Colonna, a member of a noble family of that name which had disturbed the peace of Rome for centuries. Like others of his kind, this Fabrizio had served as a mercenary commander under Spain's 'Catholic Kings' – Ferdinand and Isabella – during their wars in northern Italy. Now he is travelling back to his native Rome and, stopping in Florence, ready to hold forth on his experiences.

During his years in office (1498–1512) Machiavelli himself had been in charge of conducting Florence's war against Pisa. The conflict dragged on and on, and to save money Machiavelli at one point persuaded the *signoria* to supplement the mercenaries doing the fighting with conscripted inhabitants of Florence's own *contado* or countryside. The experiment, the subject of much scepticism, worked and Pisa was duly taken. Not long after, however, the same troops scattered to the

The 'Catholic Kings', Spain's Ferdinand and Isabella, were much admired by Machiavelli for their prowess in turning Spain into the strongest power in the world.

four winds in the face of Emperor Maximilian's hard-bitten mercenaries. As the Medicis, expelled in 1494, returned, Florence's republican government fell and Machiavelli himself was briefly imprisoned and tortured.

Nothing daunted, eight years later Machiavelli put his predilection for conscripts into the mouth of Fabrizio Colonna. The common opinion, which had it that civilians could not be successful soldiers, was wrong. 'My Romans' during the Republic (both in this work and in others Machiavelli all but ignored the Imperial period) had been the best soldiers in the world; since they had consisted of conscripts, so ought others in the 'modern' age. Having thus proven the superiority of conscripts to his own satisfaction, Machiavelli proceeds to describe their selection, training, discipline, equipment, marching order, methods of castrametation and the like. All of this was to be done in the Roman manner, partly as could be culled from Livy but mainly as described by Vegetius, even though Vegetius himself belonged to the late Imperial period rather than to the Republican one which Machiavelli so much admired.

Having shown what good soldiers his imaginary Romans were, Machiavelli draws them up for an equally imaginary battle. They are armed with a mixture of Greek and Roman weapons; since the formations he suggests are hopelessly out of date, to prevent them from being blown to pieces he must first of all pretend that artillery is of little use. Having done so – even at the risk of having his audience laugh at him, as he admits – he is now in a position where he can dispense some useful advice: 'In the midst of battle to confuse the hostile army, it is necessary to make something happen that will bewilder them, either by announcing some reinforcement that is coming or by showing something that appears like it.' 'When a general wins, he ought with all speed to follow up his victory.' A commander 'should never fight a battle if he does not have the advantage, or if he is not compelled by necessity'. 'The greatest and most important matter that a general should attend to is to have near him faithful men, very skilful in war and prudent, with whom he continually advises.' 'When either hunger or other natural necessity or human passion has brought your enemy to complete desperation … you ought to avoid battle so far as is in your power.' These and similar pearls of wisdom are provided with plentiful illustrations, most of them taken from the ancient world; after all, if 'Roman consuls' such as Minucius Rufus and Acilius Glabrio (who fought against Hannibal and Antiochus respectively) could do it, why not we?

Thus three of Machiavelli's key propositions – his underestimation of artillery, his recommendation that pikes be supplemented with swords and bucklers, and his preference for citizen-soldiers over professionals – proved to be dead wrong. The last of these ideas even compelled him to strike some decidedly unMachiavellian attitudes. As, for example, when he claims that professional soldiers could not be 'good men', a claim which, when put into the mouth of a man who was himself a professional soldier, forced him to turn some strange intellectual somersaults. It also compelled him to pretend that Roman military

Soldiers of Machiavelli's time, shown in this etching by Dürer.

prowess ended around the time of the Gracchi and devote but little attention to the exploits of a Marius, a Sulla, a Pompey or a Caesar, let alone other Roman commanders who had the misfortune to live during the Imperial period.

Why Machiavelli's work attained the fame that it did remains a mystery. Though none of his contemporaries took his advice with regard to conscription, they seem to have appreciated his emphasis on discipline and order. He obviously had a good understanding of the differences among the armies of his day, but his discussion of this topic is of interest only to the kind of military historian who takes the Renaissance as his speciality and wants to know, for example, how the Imperial horse differed from the French and Spanish ones. Many of his concrete suggestions are sensible enough, but lacking in originality as they are taken almost entirely from Livy, Frontinus and Vegetius (not knowing Greek, and preferring the Roman legion to the Greek phalanx, he placed much less reliance

on the remaining ancient authors). An underlying philosophy of war may be discerned in his insistence that rich and well-ordered states cannot exist without strong defences; in *The Prince* he says that 'a just war is a necessary war', thus cutting through the Gordian knot formed by endless medieval discussions of just war from Saint Augustine to Saint Thomas Aquinas. The reason for including him in these pages is principally because he is *there* and because in other respects he is a commanding intellectual figure. Like a major general standing in the middle of the road, one must salute him whether one wants to or not.

In truth, much of the remaining military thought produced between the time of Machiavelli and the French Revolution is even less impressive. Why this should be the case is not easy to say: certainly Gustavus and Turenne, Marlborough, Prince Eugène of Savoy, Maurice de Saxe and Frederick the Great deserve to be included in the list of great commanders. Yet even as they fought their various

In claiming that artillery was of little use (its cannon balls, he says, usually went high), Machiavelli may have been thinking of contraptions like this one. He was wrong, however, since sixteenth-century artillery was effective, and getting more so.

campaigns, military thought continued to draw on 'the ancients', taking their works as the acme of wisdom and contributing little themselves that was fundamentally new. To cite but one extreme example, when the Marquis de Folard wrote a famous essay on tactics in the 1720s, he cast it entirely in the form of a commentary on Polybios and, specifically, the (unsuccessful) pitting of Macedonian phalanx against Roman legion, even to the point where he treated the musket, now fixed with the newly invented bayonet, almost as if it were simply some sort of pike.

After Machiavelli, the first writer whose *oeuvre* must be discussed on these pages is Raimondo Montecuccoli. An Italian who served the Habsburgs continuously from the beginning of the Thirty Years War to his death in 1680, he somehow found the time to take an interest in every aspect of the intellectual life of his times, including, not least, the occult. His most important work was the *Treatise on War*, which was written in 1639–43 when he was a prisoner of the Swedes; however, it was apparently regarded as a state secret and, though allowed to circulate in

73

NICOLAI
MACHIAVELLI
PRINCEPS.

EX
SYLVESTRI TELII
FVLGINATIS TRADVCTIONE
diligenter emendata.

Adiecta sunt eiusdem argumenti, Aliorum quorundam
contra Machiauellum scripta de potestate &
officio Principum, & contra tyrannos.

BASILEAE
Ex officina Petri Pernæ.
M D XXC.

The cover of Machiavelli's
The Prince, *Latin edition,*
Basel, 1580.

manuscript form, was published only long after his death. Foreshadowing the Enlightenment, Montecuccoli's objective was to investigate every part of the art of war from observation and experience. Next he proposed to draw up detailed rules, and join them into a system which would be subject to reason.

Accordingly, part 1 discusses preparations for war, including political preparations: the striking of alliances and the amassing of supplies, arms and money. Part 2 deals with training, discipline, logistics and intelligence; unlike Machiavelli, Montecuccoli was a firm

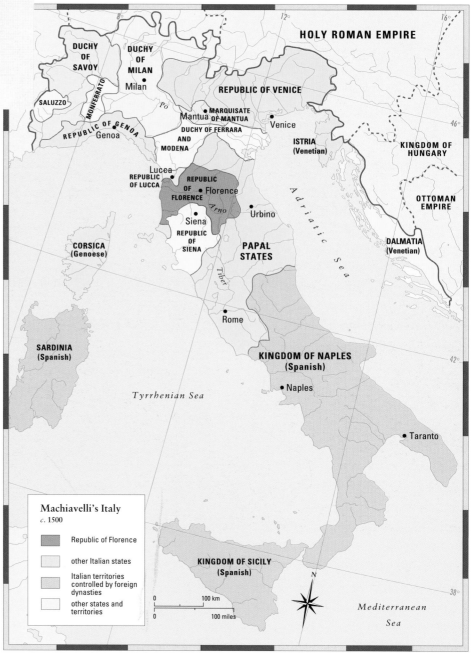

MACHIAVELLI'S ITALY

During Machiavelli's time Italy was divided between numerous city states, large and small. Some were republics, but the majority were ruled by tyrants. Against this political background Machiavelli's proposals for a citizen army made no sense.

advocate of standing professional forces of the kind which had been pioneered by the Dutch general, Maurice of Nassau. This part also has much to say about the conduct of war, including fortification, marches, operational manoeuvre – a field in which Montecuccoli was considered a master – and the peculiar tactical difficulties that resulted from the need to combine cavalry with artillery and infantry, muskets with pikes. Finally, part 3 deals with what we today would call 'war termination' and the attainment of a more favourable peace.

A point which is worth making here, and which distinguishes Montecuccoli from previous writers, is that he looks at war as something made by states rather

When the Marquis de Folard wrote a famous essay on tactics in the 1720s, he cast it entirely in the form of a commentary on Polybios, as if no two-thousand-year interval separated them. The picture shows the battle of Eryx (Sicily), 248 BC, used by Folard to illustrate Polybios.

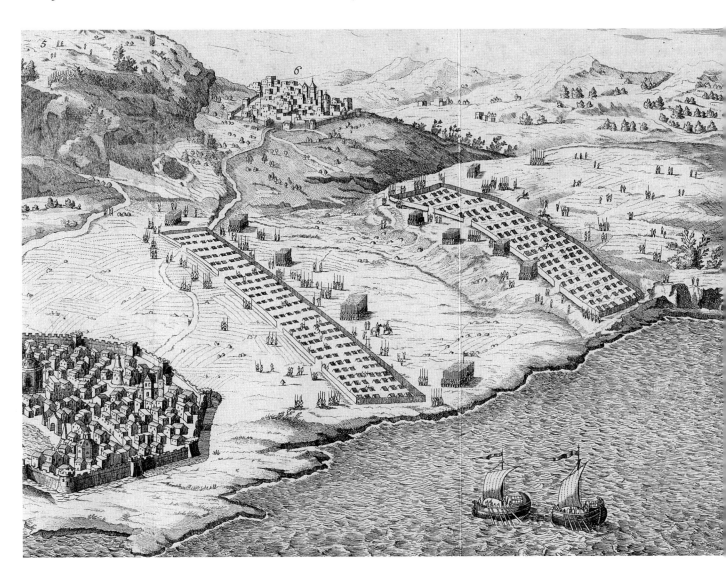

than by peoples (as in classical Greek and Republican Rome) or rulers (as in China, Imperial Rome, Byzantium, the Middle Ages and the Renaissance). Explicitly following the ideas of the late sixteenth-century political scientist Justus Lipsius, he clearly distinguishes between external and internal war; and indeed the point was soon to come where the latter no longer counted as war at

The Italian-born Raimondo Montecuccoli was the first to distinguish internal from external war. By so doing, he made a decisive contribution that led straight to Clausewitz's 'continuation of politics by other means'.

*The Thirty Years War
(1618–48) formed the
background to the military
thought of Raimondo
Montecuccoli. The
illustration shows the battle
of Fleurus (1622).*

The background to the Thirty Years War was formed by the political ideas of Justus Lipsius (second from right). The picture is by Peter Paul Rubens.

all but was downgraded to civil war, revolution, uprising and, in our own day, terrorism. To use a term I have coined elsewhere, the age of trinitarian warfare – government against government, regular army against regular army, with the people reduced to a passive role – had dawned. A century or so after Montecuccoli wrote, Frederick the Great said that Lipsius was hopelessly antiquated and should be thrown out of the window. That, however, was precisely because the Flemish philosopher's ideas on the state as the only legitimate war-making organization were now being taken very much for granted.

Much like his predecessors, Montecuccoli still failed to distinguish between strategy, the operational level and tactics. As has been well said, during most of

its history war consisted mainly of an extended walking tour combined with large-scale robbery. Deficient communications prevented the co-ordination of forces unless they were kept closely together, whereas the short range of weapons meant that active hostilities against the enemy could only get under way on those comparatively rare occasions when armies drew up opposite each other so as to give battle. Though statesmen such as Pericles and commanders-in-chief such as Hannibal clearly had in mind some master plans by which they sought to achieve victory, if we look for the above-mentioned distinctions in any of the writings discussed so far, we will do so in vain. Towards the end of Montecuccoli's life the term 'tactics', derived from the Greek and meaning the ordering of formations on

The Spanish road – the Habsburg Empire

During the sixteenth century Spanish commanders were almost always ahead of those of other nations in the development of tactics, the introduction of small arms and in the development of artillery weapons. This was funded by the wealth supplied by the gold and silver mines of Spain's American empire and transformed into troops and equipment deployed to support her European ambitions.

the battlefield, was just beginning to come into usage. However, another century had to pass before it was clearly distinguished from strategy in the sense of the conduct of war at the higher level.

To a man, Montecuccoli's eighteenth-century successors continued to write as if tactics, operational art and strategy were one. To a man, too, they accepted the idea that war was something to be conducted against foreigners in a different, normally but not invariably neighbouring, country. Finally, to a man they shared his notion that the purpose of theory was to reduce warfare to a 'system' of rules which would be grounded in experience and supported by reason. Obviously this was something that was much easier to do in regard to fields where the enemy's independent will did not have to be taken into consideration. Thus discipline, marches, logistics and cantonments were easier to encompass than were tactics, tactics easier than operational art, and operational art easier than strategy. Hence, as Clausewitz later noted, from about 1690 on there was a tendency for

THE CASTLE

As a focal point of power the castle or fort developed from its original rudimentary mound and wooden palisades into stone towers, walls and keeps of various designs.

With the advent of gunpowder the fort adopted new forms of defence in order to present a minimum profile and walls of maximum thickness to withstand cannon fire.

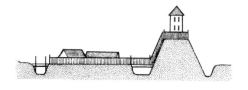

MOTTE AND BAILEY TIMBER FORT, AD 900

MEDIEVAL STONE CURTAIN-WALLED CASTLE, 1200

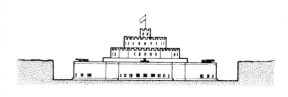

FORTRESS FROM THE ADVENT OF ARTILLERY, 1600

theory to grow from the bottom up, so to speak. It started with the most technical operations and, expanding its horizons, progressed towards greater things.

With Montecuccoli having pointed out the things which military theory ought to aim at, the first part of the art of war to be reduced to a 'system' was, as might be expected, siege warfare. Since the end of the fifteenth century and the beginning of the sixteenth, a period which saw the introduction of the first effective siege artillery on the one hand and of the bastion on the other, both the art of attacking fortresses and that of defending them had made great strides; by the late seventeenth century the acknowledged master in both fields was a Frenchman, Sébastien le Prestre de Vauban (1633–1707). Of bourgeois origins, a military engineer who spent his life alternately building fortifications for Louis XIV or conducting sieges in that king's name, Vauban put down his experiences in two slim volumes which dealt with the defence and the attack, respectively. His

Since the end of the fifteenth century the art of attacking and defending fortresses had made great strides; later, it was to be reduced to a system by such experts as Vauban, who also wrote the most famous treatise about it. Measures taken in defence of a city, woodcut by Albrecht Dürer.

OPPOSITE: *Paris city gate, built by Vauban to combine the requirements of defence with those of aesthetics.*

work neither was nor claimed to be a comprehensive treatise on the art of war. On the other hand, and thanks largely to the fact that of all types of military operations siege warfare was the easiest to reduce to rules, it was a model of its kind which others sought to emulate. (Elsewhere, Vauban was less narrow-minded. As he wrote, having done so much to diminish the members of the human race he would now do something for their propagation, and produced a treatise on increasing the number of France's inhabitants.)

The precise ways in which Vauban recommended that fortresses be attacked or defended do not concern us here. Suffice it to say that, in both respects, he proposed an extremely methodical *modus operandi* designed to achieve the objective step by step and with as few casualties – the king's professional soldiers were expensive to raise, equip and maintain – as possible. Focusing on the attack, the first step was to concentrate an army as well as sufficient supplies of everything needed: including, besides the men and their arms, ammunition, powder (also for putting in mines), engineering materials and tools. Then it was

Vauban, author of works on defence and attack, planning the fortifications of Belfort, 1678.

Caserne A

necessary to isolate the soon-to-be-taken fortress by isolating it from the outside world, using lines of vallation and countervallation for the purpose. Next a thorough reconnaissance made by the commander in person was to reveal the fortress's weak points. The guns were to be brought up, properly situated and dug in. The bombardment itself was to be carried out in three bounds as each bound brought the attackers closer to the walls. Sallies by the defenders were to be carefully guarded against and, if they took place nevertheless, allowed to run their course and be repulsed before siege operations properly speaking resumed. Breaches were to be systematically widened until they were 'practicable'. And so

on, measure for measure, until the capture – or, even better, the surrender – of the fortress was obtained.

Lately, attempts have been made to belittle Vauban's originality and deny his historical importance both as a builder and as a commander. Be this as it may, the fact remains that his writings have never been surpassed in their own field. As late as 1830 they were still being reprinted as a practical guide; meanwhile whatever theoretical wisdom was contributed by others who were active in the field had long been forgotten. The aim of his successors, one and all, was to extend his approach to warfare in its entirety, a task in which they invariably failed. To pass over them rapidly, Jacques François de Chastenet, Marquis de Puysegur (1655–1743), spent most of his life fighting for Louis XIV, in whose army he finally rose to the position of quartermaster-general. Written in the 1720s, his *L'Art de la guerre par des principes et des règles* (The Art of War by Principles and Rules) was explicitly modelled on Vauban; what the latter had done for siege warfare Puysegur sought to do for 'the entire theory of war from the smallest part to the largest'. Seeking to contradict those who claimed that only practice mattered, moreover, he wanted to show that war could be taught 'without war, without troops, without an army, without having to leave one's home, simply by means of study, with a little geometry and geography'.

Having provided a survey of ancient and modern military writers as well as his own military experience, Puysegur explains that 'the foundation of the art of war is knowing how to form good *ordres de bataille* and how to make them move and operate according to the most perfect rules of movement; the principles of which are derived from geometry, which all officers must be familiar with'. Applying his own recipe step by step, he then illustrates the use of geometrical principles in order to find 'the best method' for (*inter alia*) conducting marches, carrying out manoeuvres in the face of the enemy, constructing camps, confronting an enemy who may have taken shelter behind lines, rivers, marshes, inundations, woods and other obstacles, as well as foraging and passing convoys. Having done all this he concludes with 'the movements of two armies advancing upon

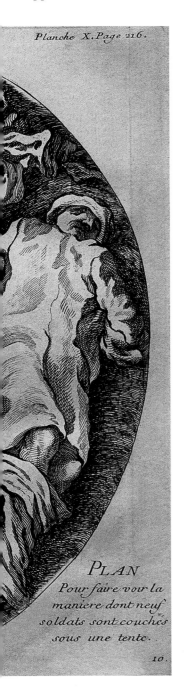

Planche X.Page 216.

PLAN
Pour faire voir la manière dont neuf soldats sont couchés sous une tente.

10.

Soldiers asleep; an illustration from Puysegur's L'Art de la Guerre.

each other', breaking off his near-endless catalogue of 'principles and rules' precisely at the point where war, here understood as an *interaction* of the two sides, begins.

More famous than Puysegur was Maurice, also known as Marshal de Saxe (1696–1750). A natural son of the Elector of Saxony, he became a professional soldier and rose to become commander-in-chief of the French army during the war of the Austrian Succession (1740–48). He produced his *Rêveries* (Dreams) in 1732, allegedly during thirteen feverish nights and with no other aim in mind except that of amusing himself. On one level the book is a reaction against Puysegur; it starts by lamenting the absence of any reference to the

'sublime' (i.e. non-mechanical) aspects of war in his predecessor's work. On another level it epitomizes eighteenth-century warfare at its complex best, assuming as it does two comparatively small armies (at one point, following Montecuccoli, he says that 50,000 is the maximum that can be handled by any general) manoeuvring against each other with the aim of fulfilling the sovereign's orders to capture this province or that. This manoeuvring was seen as the essence of war; battle was to be engaged in only as a last resort, and then only when the prospects for victory appeared certain. There are separate chapters about field warfare, mountain warfare, siege warfare, and the problems of building field fortifications and dealing with them. Unlike many of his contemporaries,

Mes Rêveries, *by Marshal de Saxe, was a famous eighteenth-century treatise on the art of war. The picture shows the author after his greatest victory, won at Fontenoy in 1745.*

OPPOSITE: 'France under Louis XV was governed by a cabal of four plus Madame de Pompadour.' Painting by François Drouais, 1763–4.

moreover, de Saxe as a foreign nobleman without an independent fortune had worked his way up the chain of command almost from the bottom. Hence he also had many shrewd observations concerning the need to keep the soldiers' clothing simple and the commander's mind free of excessive detail; not to mention the danger of making generals out of mere colonels and thus risking the possibility that, following the Peter Principle, they would find themselves one step above their natural ability.

Generally, though, his most important contribution is considered to be the 'legion'. Against the background of a period that still did not possess integrated formations comprising all arms – the largest unit was the regiment – de Saxe proposed the establishment of such formations, each one numbering exactly 3,582 men and comprising, besides four infantry regiments, four troops of horse (one for each regiment), two twelve-pounder guns, a permanent headquarters, transport, engineers and various supporting services. With that the need to draw up a detailed *ordre de bataille*, which Puysegur had regarded as the very essence of the military art, for each occasion would be obviated. One would simply be able to name a 'legion' and send it on this mission or that; in addition, permanent formations would prove to be more cohesive than the rest and would thus be able to serve as 'a kind of universal seminary of soldiers where different nations are freely adopted and their natural prejudices effectually removed'. In the event the idea of building large, permanent, combined formations was destined to be adopted during the second half of the century and proved critical to the development of the art of war and of strategy in particular. Still, no more than his contemporaries did de Saxe himself distinguish between strategy and tactics.

To round off this chapter, the military works of Frederick the Great must be briefly discussed. Reflecting the typical Enlightenment belief in education, they were produced over a period of some thirty years. First came the *Principes généraux* of 1746; this was followed by the *Testament politique* (1761), the *Testament militaire* (1768) and the *Eléments de castrametrique et de tactique* (1771), as well as a long didactic poem known as *The Art of War*. Much of this material was originally secret and intended strictly for the use of senior Prussian officers and officials. Accordingly it does not deal so much with the art of war *per se* as the way in which it ought to be practised by Prussia, and again the reason for including it here is mainly the fact that its author was undoubtedly one of the greatest commanders of all time.

Prussia, then, is described as an artificial country, spread over much of Germany and Poland, and held together as a work of art. At the centre of the work was the army, which alone could guarantee its continued existence and which accordingly had to be fostered by all means. For both military and political reasons the army's commander was to be the king alone; not for Frederick the *conseils de guerre* which were common elsewhere and for which he frequently expressed his contempt, commenting for example that France under Louis XV

was governed by a cabal of four plus Madame de Pompadour. The officers were to be drawn exclusively from the nobility: 'the one factor which can make men march into the cannon that are trained at them is honour', and honour was to be found among nobles alone. While not incapable of putting on a show of gruff appreciation for the rank and file, Frederick believed that the one way to keep them in line was ferocious discipline. 'They need to fear their officers more than the enemy,' he once commented.

Held together by iron bonds, such an army would be able to march more rapidly, manoeuvre more precisely, and fire more rapidly than the enemy. Above all, it would be able to take casualties, recover from defeat and fight again –

Under Frederick the Great, Prussian soldiers were supposed to 'fear their officers more than the enemy'. A Prussian army camp, mid eighteenth century.

a most important factor considering the number of battles which Frederick lost. With these rock-solid elements in place, he could instruct his generals about the details. Thus during marches the army's two wings were not to be separated by more than a few miles. Provisions were to be obtained by 'eating everything there is to eat [in a province] and then moving somewhere else'. Mountains, swamps, forests and other places capable of offering shelter to deserters were to be avoided as far as possible, and foraging soldiers were to be carefully guarded. The best method of espionage, 'which always succeeds', was to choose a peasant, arrest his wife as a hostage, and attach to him a soldier disguised as a servant before sending him into the enemy's camp – an idea which could equally well have come

from some Chinese or Byzantine manual. He also has something to say about the use of artillery and cavalry and about the capture of defended places. Much of what he does say is incisive and succinct. Limited as it is to his own time and place, however, little of it deserves to be studied by way of a theoretical introduction to war.

Around the end of the nineteenth century, by which time the king had come to be celebrated as the founder of the Prussian–German army and any military action had to be traceable to him in order to gain respect, much ink was spilt over the question as to whether he preferred annihilation (*Niederwerfung*) to attrition (*Ermattung*) or the other way round. In fact his written works do not have very much to say about the matter; instead, his views must be deduced from his practice. On two occasions, then, Frederick engaged in what today would be called a *Blitzkrieg*: in 1741 he sought to overrun Silesia, and in 1756 Saxony, before the enemy, in both cases Austria, could react. Each time the attempt to

Before the invention of photography commanders had to be adept at sketching. This topographical sketch was prepared by Frederick the Great in 1741 as part of his plan to invade Silesia.

annihilate the enemy, if such it was, failed and he became involved in a protracted war which even assumed pan-European dimensions. If only because two are needed for a fight, in these wars Frederick showed himself neither more nor less inclined toward fighting decisive battles than his contemporaries. Such bloodbaths were indeed frequent; but so, particularly during the latter phases of the Seven Years War, were lengthy pauses and complicated manoeuvres intended to preserve his own forces and outfox the enemy.

As has already been mentioned, several Enlightenment military writers lamented the fact that, unlike other sciences, that of war did not have any clear and universally applicable rules. One and all, their objective in writing was to provide such rules for themselves (as, like de Saxe, they often claimed), for their comrades, for their subordinates and for a wider readership. Precisely because the scope of Vauban's writing was limited – it completely ignores both the military and the political context of the fortifications and sieges with which it deals – among all these works his was by far the most successful. Recognizing no such

limitations, the rest sought to construct 'systems' which would not comprise mere handbooks but cover war as a whole.

That attempt, however, was seldom successful. While many authors had interesting things to say, with the possible exception of de Saxe and his legions they are concerned with the technicalities of their own age rather than anything that foreshadows the future. Perhaps the best that can be said for them is that, as the growing number of publications in the field proves, they both reflected and were responsible for a situation in which warfare was coming to be considered a fit subject for serious theoretical study. The age of the self-taught officer who was also an entrepreneur was drawing to an end, to be replaced by that of the soldier who was commissioned after having passed through a military academy and having been subjected to further study at one of the new staff colleges that were beginning to open their doors in Prussia and France from about 1770. In the future it was to the students and graduates of these institutions, above all, that writers on military theory were to address themselves.

CHAPTER FOUR

GUIBERT TO CLAUSEWITZ

THE SIEGE OF MINORCA, April 1756, during the Seven Years War. Despite the bastions protecting the city, the French landed and invested Port Mahon, the island's capital, while the fleet blockaded the port. Minorca surrendered on 28 May. The British Admiral John Byng's failure in his action against the French led to his court-martial and execution.

GUIBERT TO CLAUSEWITZ

IN THE MILITARY FIELD, as in others, the years leading up to the French Revolution were marked by intellectual ferment. The political system of absolute states which had been created at the Peace of Westphalia in 1648 was visibly coming apart at the seams. Both Louis XV and Frederick II were aware that radical change was on the way; and the former in particular expressed his hope that the deluge would only come '*après moi*'. The nature of the change was foreshadowed in the work of political writers, of whom the most radical was Rousseau. In the military field the writer who made the greatest name for himself was a young man named Jacques Antoine Hippolyte, Comte de Guibert.

The background to Guibert's work, like that of his late eighteenth-century contemporaries, was formed by the Seven Years War, which related to the period 1763–89 much as the First World War did to the period 1919–39, i.e. as a paradigm. In that conflict the French army had performed poorly, failing to achieve much against Frederick the Great's Prussia even though, together with its

The Peace Treaty of Westphalia, 24 October 1648, ending the Thirty Years War.

96

allies Austria and Russia, France had enjoyed every advantage, economic, numerical and geographical. Guibert *père* had participated in the Seven Years War as an assistant to the last French commander in Germany, Marshal de Broglie. The question which occupied Guibert *fils*, who ended up as a colonel in that conflict, was how to do better next time. Typically of the times in which he lived, he sought to answer the question not merely by offering specific recommendations, but by producing a grand 'system' of war which would cover the entire subject, both historically and philosophically. The *Essai tactique générale*, published in 1772 when Guibert was only twenty-nine years old, was supposed to represent that system and, at the same time, confer immortality upon its author.

Guibert's detailed recommendations concerning the shape of military formations – for example, he helped produce the ordinance of 1791 with which the French army fought the Revolutionary and Napoleonic wars – need not concern us here. Four propositions, however, are outstanding and justify the high reputation he enjoyed among his contemporaries. First, to overcome the feebleness so characteristic of France's conduct of the recent conflict, future war

PRUSSIA 1713–86

Prussia's growing military might under the leadership of Frederick the Second (Frederick the Great) alarmed her neighbours, three of which eventually mobilized armies against her.

Prussia 1713–86

Prussia 1713–40

Prussia 1740–86

Holy Roman Empire

Each symbol represents 10,000 men under arms in the period 1740–86

Prussians

Russians

Austrians

French

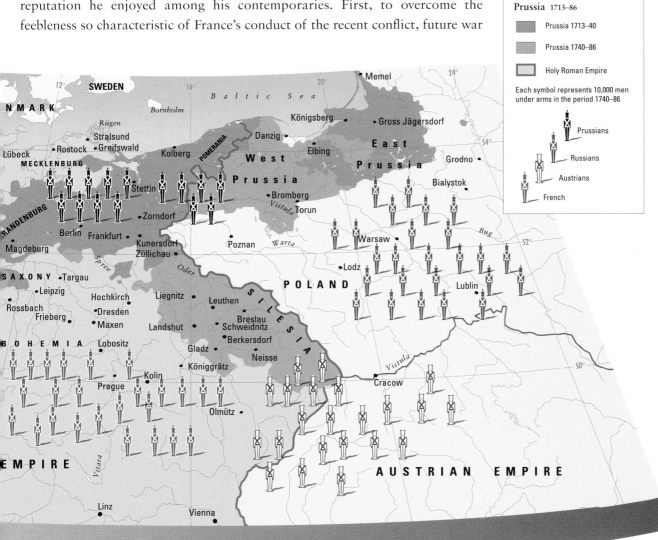

should be waged not merely with the aid of the standing army but on the basis of the united forces of the entire nation. Second, to make such participation possible, general conscription was to be introduced. Third, to enable the huge resulting armies to survive without ruining the treasury, the existing logistic system was to be reformed and war made to feed war. Fourth, those same huge armies were to move not in a single block – as had been standard practice from time immemorial to that of Frederick the Great – but in independent formations of all arms. The last-named demand clearly echoed de Saxe: but it could also rely on the French commander de Broglie who, during the latter years of the Seven Years War, was the first to conduct practical experiments with the type of unit later to be known as the division. However, what really made Guibert famous was not so much the technical details which he expounded as his implied demand for far-reaching political reform which in turn would make possible an army of a completely new kind. Backed by the mobilized nation, such an army, thanks to its numbers on the one hand and its patriotic vigour on the other, would sweep away its opponents 'like reeds before the north wind'.

War zones of the Seven Years War 1756–63

Although it was the smallest of the large powers Prussia, with just 175,000 troops and assisted only by Britain, took on the remaining great powers. Emerging from the war exhausted but triumphant, it established itself as a great power for the first time.

As will be evident from the title of his work, Guibert still did not distinguish between tactics and strategy (so it is strange to find one modern book on him subtitled 'The Voice of Strategy'). At the same time his distinction between 'elementary tactics' (the use of the various arms) and 'great tactics' (marching, combat, deployment and encamping) shows that he was groping his way towards the latter concept. Against this background the term 'strategy' was initiated during those very years by another French soldier–scholar, Joly de Maizeroy. Maizeroy too sought to put right the defects which had become apparent in the French army during the Seven Years War and, to do so, produced his own 'system'. As he defined the subject, tactics were 'merely mechanical' and included the 'composing and ordering of troops [as well as] the manner of marching, manoeuvring and fighting' as expounded by Puysegur, de Saxe and others. On the other hand, strategy was concerned with the overall conduct of military operations against the enemy – a field which hitherto had been left almost entirely to the general's intuition.

To call the conduct of war at the higher level by a new name was one thing. To devise principles for it was an entirely different matter, and one whose

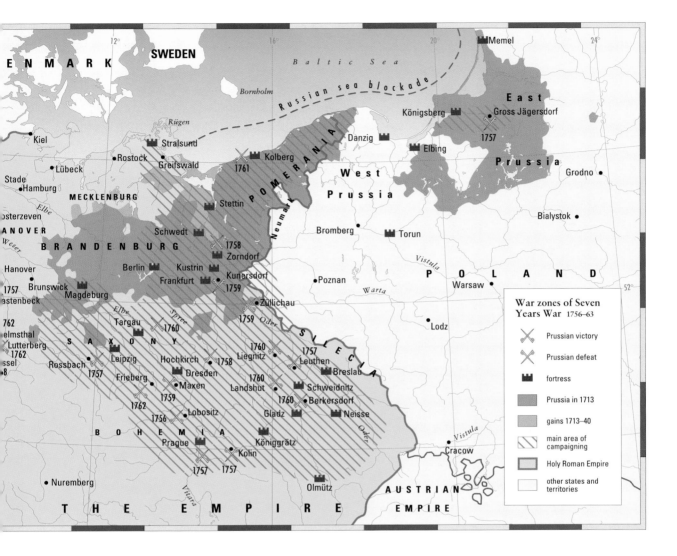

difficulty had defeated all previous writers even if, as was seldom the case before 1700 or so, they had attempted it in the first place. The credit for putting together the earliest treatise on strategy belongs to a Prussian officer and writer, Adam Heinrich Dietrich von Buelow, whose *Geist des neuern Kriegssystems* (Spirit of the Modern System of War) appeared in 1799. An eccentric, arrogant genius who had a knack for alienating people and creating enemies, Buelow's point of departure was the much improved maps which were becoming available. For example, Roman commanders had maps (to judge by the only specimen that has come down to us, the so-called *tabula peutingeriana*) in which only east and west, but not north and south, were indicated. Spanish commanders marching their forces from northern Italy to the Netherlands in the latter half of the sixteenth century had relied on mere sketches to show them the way; even Vauban, as great an expert on military geography as has ever lived, at various times produced estimates of the surface of France which differed from each other by as much as 30 per cent. However, by the time Buelow wrote, the first map of a large country (France) to be based on triangulation rather than on guesswork had just been completed and submitted to the *dépôt de guerre* in Paris, and several more works aiming to cover other countries in a similar way were approaching completion.

Strategy, then, was the art of conducting war not by means of *coup d'oeil* from behind a horse's ears but in an office, on the surface of a map. Thus regarded, any army once deployed on the border would occupy a base, conceived by Buelow not as a point but as a definite area with definite dimensions. Depending on geography and the general's decision, a base could be either narrow or wide. Starting from it, the army was to advance upon its objective or objectives; between base and objective there stretched a line, or lines, of operations. Along these lines there flowed supplies and reinforcements in one direction and the wounded, the sick and prisoners in the other. As of recent times the growing role played by firearms had greatly increased the demand for

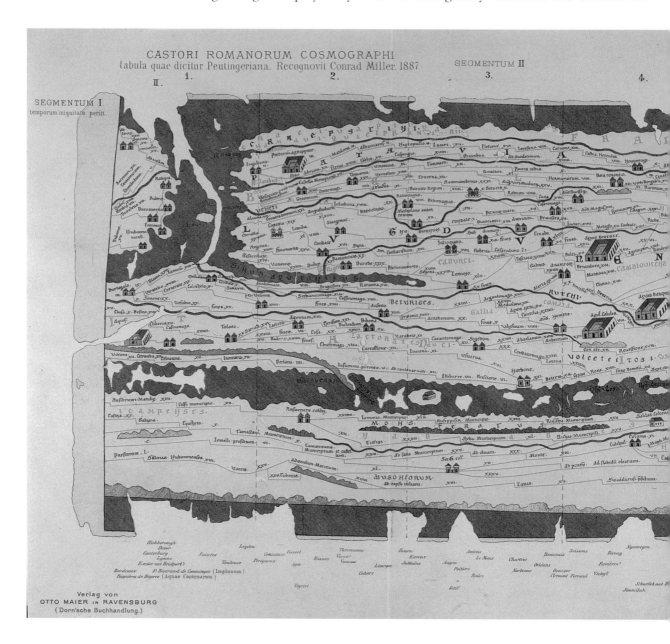

ammunition and, in this way, the importance of the lines. It was in them that the key to strategy was to be found.

For example, a general who contemplated an invasion of a neighbouring country might advance in one line, in two, or in more. Depending on the extent of the base, as well as the number and location of the objectives selected, these lines might either diverge, converge or run parallel to each other. The columns moving along each one might be made equally strong, or else different numbers of troops might be assigned to each. To obtain certainty in such questions (as in any others) it was necessary to resort to mathematics; which made Buelow's work resemble nothing so much as a textbook in Euclidean geometry. Definitions are provided and followed by propositions, which are then linked to each other by 'proofs'. Thus various possibilities, such as diverging lines and parallel lines, are

carefully eliminated. Having determined that converging lines are best, the remaining question is how far away the objective ought to be. Like the power of gravity, that of the offensive diminishes the further into enemy territory it advances. If the advancing force is not to be cut off by a flanking attack, a definite relationship should be maintained between the length of the line of operations and the width of the base. Thus two lines stretching from the flanks of the base should meet at the objective in such a way that they form a right angle. Proceed further than this – in other words, allow a sharp angle to be created – and you risk being cut off by a side-stroke. Thus the entire art of strategy was reduced to a single, simple, geometrical formula.

Though not entirely without forerunners – in particular, the British officer and writer Henry Lloyd deserves to be mentioned – Buelow was right in claiming that his system of strategy marked 'an entirely new' way of looking at war. For centuries, if not millennia, students had busied themselves with the best method for raising an army, disciplining it, arming and equipping it, building camps for it, provisioning it, adopting this or that marching order and, when it came to confronting the enemy, either fighting him or tricking him by means of this stratagem or that. However, Buelow shifted the emphasis from what we today would call the organizational, technical and tactical aspects towards the larger operations of war. No

Early maps were often primitive, providing a scant base for strategy. The tabula peutingeriana *was a thirteenth-century copy of a fourth-century Roman map. The section shown here includes England, France and North Africa.*

With the invention of modern strategy towards the end of the eighteenth century, generalship ceased to be a question of coup d'oeil *and began to be conducted on a map. This is a portrait of the French general Louis-Lazare Hoche, c. 1795.*

wonder he was carried away by his own discovery. Thus, in the face of unfolding Napoleonic warfare with its numerous climactic battles, he insisted that the correct understanding and adoption of his system of strategic manoeuvres would cause battle to disappear. Given that their growing dependence on magazines and lines of operations prevented armies from proceeding very far from their base, he even expected that war itself would be recognized as futile and come to an end – not that this was a rare belief either in the years before 1789 or, more surprisingly, after 1815.

Buelow and his fellow German strategists (for some reason the term strategy caught on much faster in Germany than anywhere else) have often been ridiculed, nowhere more so than in Tolstoy's *War and Peace*. Yet the censure is undeserved: even if wars did not come to an end, his prediction that the art of strategy would work in favour of large states and lead to political consolidation proved correct. To this day, even those who have never heard of him use the concepts which he pioneered – base, objective, lines of operations – and, what is more, look at strategy in a manner which was largely his making. From then on, as far as

Following his discovery of lines of communication, Buelow expected battle to disappear. This, however, did not happen. This picture shows Napoleon issuing an ADC with orders for Marshal Grouchy at the Battle of Waterloo, 1815.

strategy on land was concerned, it only remained to work out the details. Nineteenth-century schools of strategy – i.e. the multiplying staff colleges – were soon to engage in endless arguments as to whether a single line of operations or a double one, converging or diverging, was preferable; and whether to drive forward (in other words, attack) was easier than to maintain one's base (in other words, defend). Furthermore, as we shall see, Buelow was by no means the last to try to arrange things in such a way that strategy – expressed in the form of lines or arrows on a map – would take the place of battle.

Buelow's direct, and much better-known, successor was Antoine Henri Jomini. A Swiss citizen who saw service under Napoleon and eventually rose to become chief of staff to Marshal Ney, he began his career as a military theorist by throwing his own early essays – which had been written before he discovered Lloyd and Buelow – into the fire. His military career was not a great success; yet he developed into the high priest of strategy or, as he himself preferred to call it, *les grandes opérations de guerre*. Acknowledged or not, his influence has probably not been surpassed even by the great Clausewitz.

The Swedish king Gustavus Adolphus could never have carried out his conquests in Germany if he had been dependent on lines of communication to bring his supplies from Sweden. Here is is shown preparing for the assault at the battle of Luetzen, 16 November 1632, in which he lost his life.

MANOEUVRE ON ULM

Ulm (autumn 1805) was the first of Napoleon's greatest campaigns. It involved several corps over a large area combining operations, converging on the enemy's lines of communication and cutting them off.

Very much like Buelow, Jomini conceived strategy in terms of armed forces moving against each other in two-dimensional space. Much more than Buelow, whose mind tended to work in eighteenth-century geometrical terms, he was prepared to take into account such complicating factors as roads, rivers, mountains, forests, fortresses and the like which either facilitated manoeuvre or obstructed it. As with Buelow, the problem was to discover a 'system' which would guide a commander in conducting those manoeuvres. The most important elements of the system remained as before, i.e. bases, objectives and lines of

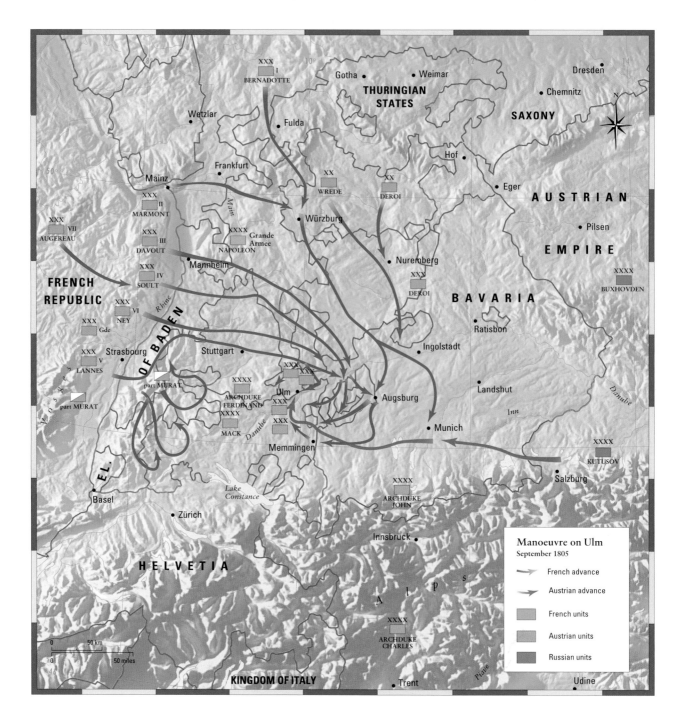

Manoeuvre on Ulm
September 1805

→ French advance

→ Austrian advance

French units

Austrian units

Russian units

operations of which there could be various numbers and which stood in various relationships to each other. To these, however, Jomini added a considerable number of other concepts. Some, such as Theatres of Operations (assuming a country engaged against multiple enemies, each of its armies would operate in a separate theatre) and Zones of Operations (the district between an army's base and its objective, through which its communications passed), were to prove useful and make their way into subsequent strategic thought. Others merely injected unnecessary complexity and, some would say, incomprehensibility.

The battle of Marengo, 14 June 1800, for the first time illustrated what la manoeuvre sur les derrières, *could do when applied on a strategic scale.*

All armies, then, necessarily had lines of operation or, as we would say today, communications. Earlier commanders such as Alexander, Julius Caesar, or even Gustavus Adolphus during the first half of the seventeenth century had been able to survive and operate for years in enemy territory while maintaining only the most tenuous ties with home. Now, however, the whole point of the art of war was to cut one's enemy's lines of operations without exposing one's own; this would lead either to the enemy's surrender (as actually happened to the Austrians at Ulm in 1805) or to a battle in which he would be placed at a grave disadvantage (as happened to the Austrians at Marengo in 1800 and to the Prussians at Jena in 1806). Thus was born the *manoeuvre sur les derrières*, a method of operation by which one part of the army would hold the enemy while the other, if possible while using some natural obstacle in order to conceal and protect itself, would march around him and fall upon his rear. As Jomini very sensibly wrote, an army with two different lines of operations running back to two different bases would be less exposed to this sort of manoeuvre than its enemy who possessed only one, particularly if the lines in question formed an obtuse angle rather an acute one. That he spoke of the theatre of war as a 'chessboard' and presented his idea in an old-fashioned geometric manner reminiscent of Buelow detracts nothing from its validity.

The second most important manoeuvre advocated by Jomini consisted of operating on

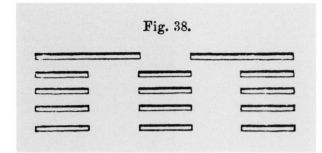

A typical illustration from one of Jomini's works, showing one of the numerous different formations that might be employed in battle.

internal (what Buelow called diverging) lines. A blue army might find itself between two red ones, as had happened to Napoleon during his Italian campaign of 1796 and again in those of 1813 and 1814 (the practice of always using blue for friendly and red for hostile originated with Helmut von Moltke). Such a situation was not without its dangers, but on the other hand it was also a source of opportunity. Separated from each other, the red forces would find it difficult to unite and thus bring superior force to bear. Conversely, the blue army was already concentrated and only a short distance away from each red force. These advantages might be used in order to deliver a swift, sharp blow at one red force before the other could intervene; after which blue would turn around and the process would be repeated against the other. A perfect example, and one which shows the continuing relevance of Jomini even in the age of air warfare which he never contemplated, is Israel's conduct of the 1967 war against three Arab

The campaign of 1806, culminating in the battle of Jena, represented the manoeuvre sur les derrières *at its most effective.*

enemies, each of which, being separated from the rest by long and tenuous lines of communications, was attacked and defeated in its turn.

Whatever the precise manoeuvre selected, it was always a question of bringing superior force to bear against the decisive point. Given their importance as centres of communication, capitals were always decisive points. So, to a lesser degree, were road junctions, river crossings, fortresses which blocked or dominated a road and the like. Another type of decisive point was that from which red's lines of operation could be threatened so that he either had to retreat from his positions or else had to turn around and fight. If he tried to do the second without doing the first, his forces would become divided, which in turn might present blue with an opportunity to beat them in detail.

In a certain sense the manoeuvres advocated by Jomini had always existed. From at least the time of Hannibal, armies had not only fought each other front to front but sought to outflank and surround the other. Before the middle of the eighteenth century, however, by and large there were no lines of operation to threaten or cut. Moreover, as explained earlier, primitive communications and the fact that no formations of all arms existed compelled armies to stick closely together and only permitted them to engage each other in battle by mutual consent. Given the vastly increased forces made available by the introduction of general conscription in 1793, first Carnot and then Napoleon had been compelled to disperse them and group them into formations of all arms whether they wanted to or not. Once the machinery for commanding such dispersed formations had also been created in the form of the *état-major*, these changes greatly increased the repertoire of strategic manoeuvres, which in turn were put into systematic form and codified by Jomini.

Jomini's earliest work on strategy, the *Traité des grandes opérations militaires* (Treatise on Grand Operations of War), was published in 1804–5 and submitted to Napoleon who, according to its author, is said to have expressed his appreciation. (Elsewhere, however, Napoleon expressed his disdain for Jomini, saying that one could turn to him if one needed an explanation concerning the nature of lines of operations, etc.) From now on he steadily added to it, without, however, changing the essence. In his most mature work, *Précis de l'art de la guerre* (The Art of War) of 1830, he has much to say about the political uses to which war could be put and also about the resources and military institutions of different states; at the same time he extends the work to include formations, tactics, various kinds of special operations such as the crossing of rivers, and logistics, defined as 'the practical art of moving armies'. There is even a short chapter on 'Descents, or Maritime Expeditions'. Therefore, if Clausewitz in *Vom Kriege* (On War) of 1833 accused Jomini of having concentrated merely on strategy to the detriment of the political side of war, this is due to the fact that the Prussian general did not live to see his rival's most mature work.

More to the point, Jomini, like all his Enlightenment predecessors, sought to create a 'system' which would tell a commander how to conduct war on the higher level. Particularly in his earlier works, this objective forced him to present war as more rational than it really is, given that only the rational can be systematically analysed, systematized and taught. The same was even more true of the Enlightenment as a whole. From about 1770 on, this view came under attack at the hand of the nascent romantic movement, which insisted that the emotions of the heart, not the calculations of the merely mechanical brain, stood at the centre of human life. In the military field the most important critic was yet another Prussian officer, diplomat and scholar, Georg Heinrich von Berenhorst.

Published in three volumes between 1796 and 1799, Berenhorst's *Betrachtungen über die Kriegskunst* (Reflections on the Art of War) began with a survey of military history. Antiquity had been the great period when the art of war, emerging from its primitive stage where it had been confined to raids, ambushes, skirmishes and the like, had been perfected. Then came a long medieval interval marked by nothing but ignorance and disorder; but at some point between Machiavelli and Montecuccoli (Berenhorst had in mind Maurice of Nassau, the early seventeenth-century Dutch commander) order was restored and progress resumed. The very nature of their quest, however, had led all subsequent authors to overestimate the role of immutable laws while underestimating that of the unknown, uncontrollable forces of human will and emotion. Soldiers were more than robots who could fire so and so many rounds a minute; an army was not simply a machine moving along this axis or that and carrying out evolutions as its commander directed. It was the ever-variable, often unpredictable, state of mind of commanders and troops, and not simply calculations pertaining to time, distance and the angles between lines of operations, which governed victory and defeat – to say nothing about the role played by that great incalculable, pure chance.

These arguments were illustrated by referring to Frederick the Great. To the majority of late eighteenth-century commentators the king was perhaps *the* greatest commander of recent times whose manoeuvres, particularly the famous 'oblique approach' in which one wing attacked the enemy while the other was kept back, were assiduously studied. (One commentator who was not misled was Napoleon. While second to none in his admiration for the king, he claimed that the spectacle of foreigners studying the evolutions of the Prussian army made him 'laugh up his sleeve'.) Berenhorst, however, pointed to the fact that during some ten years of active operations in three wars (the first, second and third Silesian wars) those manoeuvres had been carried out no more than two or three times. Those few and far-apart occasions aside, Frederick was primarily a drill-master who time after time forced his troops into murderous battles. Those battles were won – if they were won, for Frederick's defeats were about as numerous as his victories – only by virtue of iron discipline and sheer force of will.

Well written and provided with plentiful examples, Berenhorst's work was extremely popular during the years immediately after 1800. He and Jomini formed opposite poles. The one emphasized the rational conduct of war at the

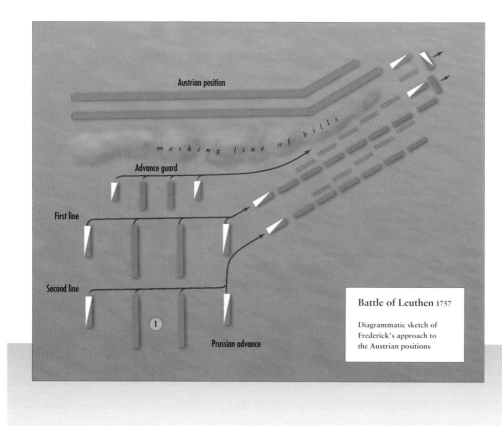

Austrian position

masking line of hills

Advance guard

First line

Second line

Prussian advance

① ①

BATTLE OF LEUTHEN 1757

The battle of Leuthen, 1757, represented eighteenth-century warfare at its superb best. Marching with machine-like precision, the Prussian army attacked one wing of an Austrian army twice its own strength. The outcome established Frederick the Great's military reputation for all time.

Battle of Leuthen 1757

Diagrammatic sketch of Frederick's approach to the Austrian positions

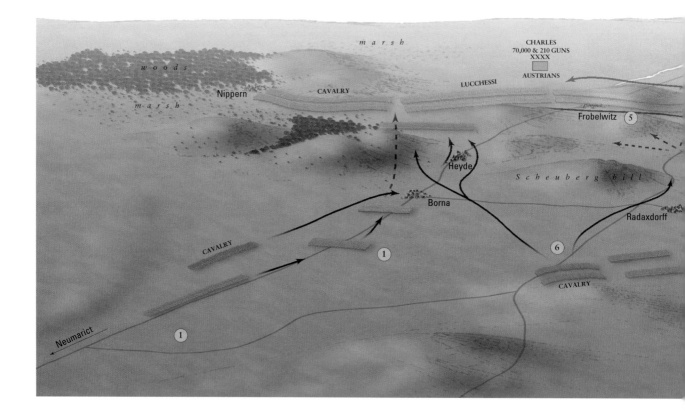

marsh

woods

marsh

Nippern

CAVALRY

LUCCHESSI

CHARLES
70,000 & 210 GUNS
XXXX
AUSTRIANS

Frobelwitz ⑤

Heyde

Scheuberg hill

Borna

Radaxdorff

CAVALRY

①

⑥

Neumarict

①

CAVALRY

hand of the strategist; the other, its essential irrationality, unpredictability and dependence on chance. Both strands of thought were to be united in the greatest of all Western writers on war, Karl von Clausewitz. Given that he too was a child of his times and went through the same tumultuous events as everyone else, it is not easy to say exactly what qualified him for playing this role. In the production of military theory, as in so many other aspects of life, room ought to be left for genius.

Clausewitz's own life has been told so many times that we can all but skip it here. The essential point is that while in his mid-twenties this unusually earnest and well-read officer began to take a serious interest in military theory. There followed his participation in the disastrous campaign of 1806, a period spent as a prisoner of war in France, and an appointment to the General Staff in Berlin where he helped Scharnhorst, his revered master, rebuild the Prussian army. By 1811 his talents as a theoretician were already sufficiently well known for him to be entrusted with teaching the Crown Prince (later, Friedrich Wilhelm IV) about

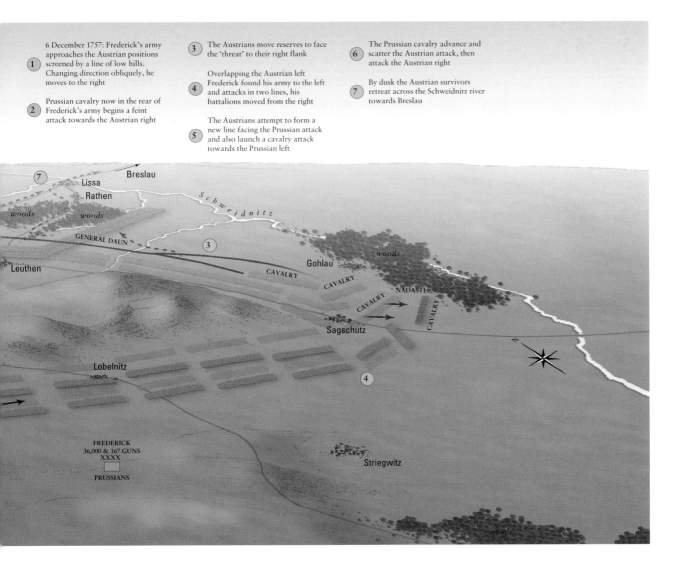

1 6 December 1757: Frederick's army approaches the Austrian positions screened by a line of low hills. Changing direction obliquely, he moves to the right

2 Prussian cavalry now in the rear of Frederick's army begins a feint attack towards the Austrian right

3 The Austrians move reserves to face the 'threat' to their right flank

4 Overlapping the Austrian left Frederick found his army to the left and attacks in two lines, his battalions moved from the right

5 The Austrians attempt to form a new line facing the Prussian attack and also launch a cavalry attack towards the Prussian left

6 The Prussian cavalry advance and scatter the Austrian attack, then attack the Austrian right

7 By dusk the Austrian survivors retreat across the Schweidnitz river towards Breslau

Vom Kriege.

Hinterlassenes Werk

des

Generals Carl von Clausewitz.

Erster Theil.

C.H.C.

Berlin,
bei Ferdinand Dümmler.
1832.

In the work of Karl von Clausewitz both the rationality of war and its irrationality were emphasized. This made him into the greatest Western military thinker of all.

war. In 1812 he found himself fighting Napoleon in Russia. During the campaigns of 1813–15 he was active as a staff officer and in 1817 assumed administrative control of the Berlin staff college or *Kriegsakademie*. Rising to the rank of general, it was there that he produced his great work.

Like almost all other military writers since 1800, Clausewitz wanted to penetrate the secret of Revolutionary and Napoleonic warfare, which, as he and the rest saw, clearly differed from what had gone before. Some had sought that secret in the mobilization of all national resources advocated by Guibert and made possible by the Revolution, others, in the conduct of strategy as explained by Buelow and, above all, Jomini. Clausewitz, however, was not simply a thoughtful soldier but a true philosopher in uniform; while accepting that the Revolution had made it possible for war to be waged 'with the full energy of the nation', he sought to go back to first principles. This he did by focusing on two questions: what was war and what purpose did it serve? From the answers to these, and constantly checking against both military history and actual experience, he sought to deduce all the rest. His approach was therefore both deductive and inductive. He himself discusses the ways in which war ought to be studied as well as the purpose which such study ought to serve. He was not to go into the details of armament and formations, let alone try to offer a solution for every problem that might arise, but to provide commanders with a basis for thought and make it unnecessary to reinvent the wheel every time. In the eyes of some, the pages which deal with this aspect of the problem are the best and most enduring part of his entire *opus*.

To answer the first question, Clausewitz in the last book of *On War* constructed an imaginary picture of 'absolute war', that is, war as it would have been if, stripped of all practical considerations concerning time, place and intent, it had been able to stand up naked, so to speak. This device, which he borrowed from contemporary physical science by way of Kant, enabled him to define war as an elemental act of violence in which all ordinary social restraints were cast off. Since force would naturally invite the use of greater force, war also possessed an inherent tendency towards escalation which made it essentially uncontrollable and unpredictable, 'a great passionate drama'. As such it was not primarily a question of acting according to this or that principle or rule; instead it represented the domain of danger, friction and uncertainty. Its successful conduct was above all a question of possessing the qualities needed in order to counter and master these inherent characteristics (where those qualities were to come from is another question, into which he refuses to enter). Not surprisingly, Clausewitz had much to say about will-power, bravery and endurance, both in the commander – whose 'genius'

The man to whom Clausewitz owed most was another Prussian staff officer, Gerhard von Scharnhorst.

By way of enhancing its prestige, the Prussian Staff College's original location was in a wing of the Charlottenburg Palace, Berlin. Clausewitz, too, lived there.

they formed – and in the army which, from top to bottom, had to be imbued with 'military virtue'. Though allowing the use of every expedient and requiring the full participation of the intellect, at bottom war was a question of character.

Much like his immediate predecessors, Clausewitz distinguished between tactics – the art of winning battles – and strategy, which he defined as the art of using battles in order to gain the objectives of the campaign. More fundamentally, though, war was a duel between two independent minds. Its interactive nature sharply differentiated it from other activities; to paraphrase, making swords (which only involved acting upon dead matter) was one thing, using them against another swordsman who is capable of parrying one's thrusts and replying with others of his own, quite another. In a brief but brilliant discussion of the theory of war, Clausewitz acknowledges that the system proffered by each of his predecessors contained an element of truth. Yet no system ought to be allowed to obscure the elemental fact that war consisted of fighting and that fighting – in other words, battle – determined the outcome of wars; no amount of fancy manoeuvring could do any good unless it was backed up with a big, sharp sword.

Furthermore, and given the high degree of uncertainty and friction involved, Clausewitz tended to belittle the effect of manoeuvre, surprise and stratagems of every kind. Trying to achieve victory by such means was all very well; but the higher the level at which war was waged, and the greater the masses which took part in it, the less likely they were to achieve decisive results. 'The best strategy is always to be very strong, first in general and then at the decisive point.' War was

'a physical and moral struggle by means of the former'. Since the enemy's strength was concentrated in his armed forces, the first objective of strategy ought always to be to smash them; this achieved, his capital could be captured and his country occupied. Thus, compared with much of what had gone before from the time of Montecuccoli onwards (and also with much of what was to come later, during the second half of the twentieth century in particular), Clausewitz's *On War* puts forward a brutally realistic doctrine, and indeed he himself says as much.

Still on the subject of strategy, and to illustrate the way Clausewitz proceeds from first principles, consider his discussion of the relationship between attack and defence, which had also occupied many earlier authors. The outstanding quality of the attack, he writes, is the delivery of a blow. The outstanding quality of the defence was the need to wait for that blow and parry it. Since anything which did not happen favoured the defence, other things being equal, to defend was easier than to attack. Moreover, the further away an attacker got from his base, the greater his logistic difficulties and the more forces he would lose owing to the need to leave behind garrisons, safeguard his communications and the like. Conversely, falling back on his base the defender would gather his forces and reinforce them. In the end, and it is here that Clausewitz shows his originality over his predecessors, inevitably there would come a 'culminating point'. The attack would turn into a defence, and the defence into an attack; that is, unless the enemy had been smashed and a decisive victory had been won first.

The battle of Leipzig, fought in November 1813, in many ways represented the culmination of French Revolutionary and Napoleonic warfare. The numbers involved, almost five hundred thousand on both sides, remained unsurpassed for half a century.

So far, he gives a brief summary of the inherent qualities of war as such. However, war was not simply a phenomenon in its own right. A product of social intercourse, it was, or at any rate ought to be, a deliberate political act, 'a continuation of policy by other means', to quote the single most celebrated phrase that Clausewitz ever wrote. It is true that war had a grammar of its own, i.e. rules which could not be violated with impunity; but it was equally true that it did not have a logic of its own. That logic was to be provided from outside, so to speak. Unless its higher conduct and general character were governed by policy, war would be 'a senseless thing, without an object'.

Translated into practical terms, this view of war as an instrument meant that ultimately its conduct had to be laid down not by the commander-in-chief but by the political leadership. What is more, it enabled Clausewitz to argue that war was morally neutral – as he says – thus once again allowing his tendency towards brutal realism to come to the fore. There can be no war without bloodshed; in dangerous things such as war, errors committed out of a feeling of benevolence are the worst. Consequently, in the entire massive work the only sentence which is devoted to the law of war is the one which says that it is so weak and unimportant as to be virtually negligible.

Towards the end of his life Clausewitz, possibly because the Napoleonic wars were slowly falling into perspective, underwent a change of mind. He now began to recognize that, besides aiming at the 'total overthrow' of the enemy – as would follow from his theoretical premises – another kind of war might be possible whose objectives were more limited. He had started to revise his work when he died of cholera, leaving behind a mass of unfinished drafts. Whether, had he lived, he would have been able to maintain his original framework or been forced to replace it with another is impossible to say. The question was, how to reconcile war's essentially unlimited nature with its use as a tool in the hand of policy; when he died, he had still not found an answer.

Among Western writers on war, the position of Clausewitz is unique. To resort to a metaphor, his is not an ordinary cookbook full of recipes concerning the utensils and ingredients which, correctly used, will yield certain foods; instead it contents itself with explaining the nature of cooking and the uses to which it is put, leaving readers to proceed on their own. As a result, when technological progress caused organization, tactics and much of strategy to change, he alone retained his relevance. While some of the details of *On War* are without enduring interest – for instance, the discussion of the relationship between the three arms and the methods for attacking a convoy – the book as a whole holds up remarkably well as 'a treasure of the human spirit'.

Thus to compare Clausewitz's advice on this or that detail with that which is proffered by his Western predecessors and contemporaries is to do him an injustice. Unlike them he was a philosopher of war; only the Chinese classics rival him in this respect, albeit that *their* underlying philosophy is radically different. Clausewitz's way of thought goes back to Aristotle and is based on the distinction between means and ends. By contrast, it is a fundamental characteristic of Chinese thought that such a distinction is absent – to Lao Tzu and his followers, admitting its existence would constitute a departure from *Tao*. Accordingly, the Chinese texts regard war not as an instrument for the attainment of this end or that but as the product of stern necessity, something which must be confronted and coped with and managed and brought to an end. As already mentioned, the only Western writer to take a similar view is Machiavelli. While Clausewitz emphasizes that war is brutal and bloody and seeks to achieve a great victory, the Chinese texts are permeated by a humanitarian approach and have as their aim the restoration of *Tao*.

These underlying philosophical differences cause Clausewitz to recommend the use of maximum force, the Chinese of minimum force. In turn, the Chinese emphasis on minimum force leads to a greater emphasis on trickery of every sort than Clausewitz, with his realistic assessment of such factors as uncertainty and friction, regards as practicable. Had the two sides met, then Sun Tzu *et al.* would undoubtedly have accused Clausewitz of overemphasizing brute strength, which in turn means encouraging stupidity and barbarism. Clausewitz on his part would have replied that the kind of super-sophisticated warfare advocated by them was intellectually attractive but, alas, often unrealistic and sometimes dangerous as excessive manoeuvring provided the enemy with opportunities to 'cut off one's head'. None of this is to deny that, in practice, Western warfare often made use of stratagems whereas Chinese warfare could be quite as bloody and brutal as its Western counterpart. Indeed, it could be more so, given that necessity has no limits and that questions regarding the law of war *à la* Bonet would have brought a contemptuous smile to the faces of the sages.

These considerations explain why Clausewitz and the Chinese were able to transcend their own time and place. Inevitably their reputations had their ups and downs. Outside China itself, where they served as the basis for the state-run examination system, the military writings were particularly popular during the eighteenth-century craze for chinoiserie, and from the 1949 Chinese Revolution on; currently there are no fewer than *four* different English translations of Sun Tzu on the market. As for Clausewitz, after being greatly venerated during the nineteenth century he was often regarded as 'too philosophical' during the first half of the twentieth. His nadir probably came during the early nuclear years when he was relegated to the sidelines, only to make an impressive comeback after 1973 when the Arab–Israeli war encouraged people to think of large-scale conventional warfare, and also when a new English translation appeared. More ups and downs are to be expected, and one recent historian even speaks of the 'grand old tradition of Clausewitz-bashing'. Yet it is likely that, when all the rest are forgotten, both Chinese military theory and Clausewitz will still be read and studied by those who seek to achieve a serious theoretical understanding of war. Which, considering that even the 'modern' Clausewitz is now almost two hundred years old, constitutes high praise indeed.

CHAPTER FIVE

THE NINETEENTH CENTURY

THE CRIMEAN WAR (1854–6) was not exactly famous for its brilliant strategy. Here Corporal Philip Smith is shown winning the Victoria Cross during the assault on Sebastopol.

THE NINETEENTH CENTURY

AN ASPECT OF CLAUSEWITZ'S THOUGHT that has not yet been discussed in these pages, and in which he differs from virtually all his predecessors, is the way history is approached. As we saw, the Chinese classics were written between 400 and 200 BC and set against the background of a semi-mythological past which was regarded as superior to the present. With the exception of Vegetius, who resembles the Chinese in this respect, in the treatises written by ancient military authors a sense of historical change is almost entirely lacking. The same is true of the Byzantine and medieval texts. Severely practical, the former are really little more than handbooks, are interested solely in the present and exclude any hint concerning the possibility that the past has been, or the future could be, different. The latter are usually aware of the glorious if idolatrous past, but somehow manage to combine this awareness with a complete disregard for the immense differences that separated their own times from those of, say, Vegetius.

The position of 'modern' Western authors from Machiavelli on is more complicated. Regarding themselves as emerging from centuries of barbarism, the men of the fifteenth century were acutely aware of their own inferiority *vis-à-vis* the ancient world in every field, the military one included. Accordingly, for them it was a question not so much of seeking for innovation as of recovering and assimilating the achievements of that world. No one was more representative of these attitudes than Machiavelli, to whom the very idea of outdoing his admired Romans would have smelt of sacrilege; but it was equally evident in his successors. Throughout the eighteenth century, most writers on military affairs insisted that the best authors to study were Frontinus and Vegetius and, among historians, Polybios, Caesar and Livy. Thus Joly de Maizeroy not only translated the Byzantine classics from the Greek but was regarded as the leading expert on ancient warfare, a subject on which he wrote several specialized studies; whereas Buelow and Berenhorst both start their works by comparing ancient warfare with that of the modern age.

And yet, even with Buelow, the situation began to change. With him this was because the ancient textbooks had absolutely nothing to say about strategy – precisely the field in which he himself made the greatest contribution and of which, understandably, he was inordinately proud. This also accounts for the fact that with Jomini, 'the ancients' are not even mentioned. Perhaps more important, however, was the overall intellectual climate in which both of them wrote. As the Enlightenment gave way to the Romantic movement, philosophers such as Vico and Hegel began promulgating a view of history which emphasized the 'otherness' of the past rather than its essential similarity with the present. Thus history, which hitherto had been a question of the same thing happening again and again (precisely *why* centuries-old events could serve as a source for practical 'lessons'), was transformed into the record of change. From now on, the further

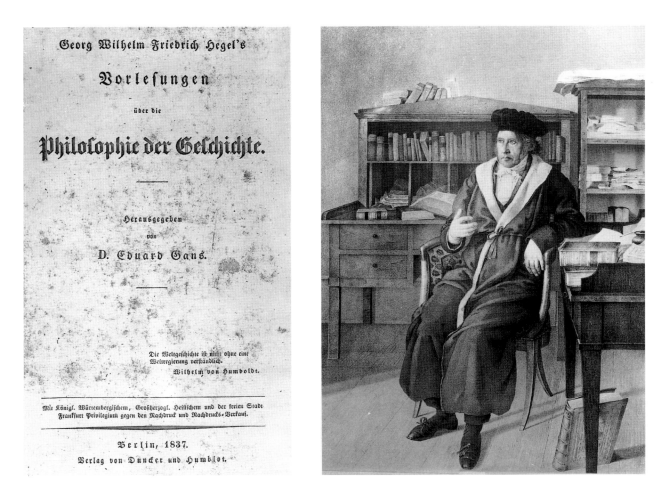

The German political scientist Georg Friedrich Hegel invented the 'otherness' of the past. By doing so, he rendered out of date all pre nineteenth-century military thought at a stroke.

back in time any period, the greater by and large the gulf that separated it from what came later on.

This is not the place to follow the transformation of history, a subject better left to specialized students of that subject. Suffice it to say that by the time Clausewitz did his main work in the 1820s it had been fully accomplished. Previously most of the authors here discussed had assumed that since history was essentially unchanging, war too had unchanging principles. Given his 'historicist' approach, however, to Clausewitz this was much less evident; in book 8 he comes very close to saying that since each period made war in a manner corresponding to its social and political characteristics, a single theory of war applicable to all times and places might not be possible at all. (Much later, interestingly enough, Mao Tse-tung quoted him on precisely this point.) Regarding himself as a practical soldier writing for other practical soldiers (the first edition of his book was sold by subscription), he was in some doubt as to how far back one could go in one's quest for rules, lessons, principles and examples; whether, in other words, 'modern' history began with the campaigns of Frederick the Great, or with the end of the war of the Spanish Succession, or with the Peace of Westphalia, which had marked the construction of the modern European state. In any case there was no doubt in his mind that, since only recent events were at all like the present, the further back one went, the less useful the things that one could find. His own writings on military history only go as far back as Gustavus Adolphus; previous wars, such as those of the Tartars and the Middle Ages, are mentioned only in order to emphasize their 'otherness'. As to the ancient authors, they are entirely ignored and none of them is even allowed to make his appearance on the pages of *On War*.

Even without the contemporary revolution in historical thought, it was becoming all too clear that the old and trusted methods for thinking about war would no longer do. Between 217 BC, when Ptolemy IV had confronted Antiochus III at Raffia, and Waterloo in 1815 the number of men who had opposed each

Owing to the fact that pikes were abandoned for the first time, the War of the Spanish Succession is sometimes taken as the beginning of 'modern' military history. This shows the battle of Cassano, Italy, 1705.

other had scarcely grown. (An exception, and one which was to prove significant for the future, was the battle of Leipzig in 1813.) It is true that, at some point located approximately three-quarters of the way from the first to the second of these battles, firearms in the form of muskets and cannon had largely taken over from edged weapons. Even so, battle remained very much what it had always been: a question of men standing up, at a certain carefully defined time and space (battles tended to be over in a few hours and seldom took up more than a few square kilometres), in relatively tight formations (throughout the eighteenth century there had been an intense debate on the relative merits of the column versus the line) and fighting one another in full view of the other. Thus Napoleon

towards the end of his career was able to boast of having commanded no fewer than sixty 'pitched battles' (*batailles rangées*), a phrase that speaks for itself.

By the middle of the nineteenth century these parade-like occasions were becoming increasingly obsolete. New, quick-firing weapons were beginning to make their appearance from about 1830, causing the amount of fire-power produced per unit and per minute to leap upwards as well as leading to dramatic improvements in accuracy and range. These developments made it questionable whether men would still be able to fight while standing on their feet and confronting each other in a relatively tight formation. As one might expect, a period of experimentation followed, nowhere more so than in the United States. There, during the Civil War, commanders who had never previously been in charge of large units, and amateurish troops who were less bound to the past than many of their professional colleagues across the Atlantic, did not hesitate to break formation, seek shelter and adopt camouflage clothing when they thought it could save their lives. Confining our view to written military thought, however, one of the first and most important authors who attempted to come to grips with the new phenomenon was a French officer, Charles-Jean-Jacques Ardant du Picq (1821–70).

In one sense, as du Picq himself says, his work represented a reaction against the geometrical approach of Buelow and Jomini. Conversely, though he does not mention them, he followed Berenhorst and Clausewitz in that he considered that the key to war was to be found not in any clever manoeuvres, let alone geometrical formulae, but in the heart of man. Much more than Clausewitz in particular, who served explicit warning against indulging in mere idle talk about the last-named subject, he was prepared to try to look into the factors which rendered that heart at least partly immune to the terror of battle. (Having seen considerable active service in the Crimea, Syria and Algeria, du Picq was under no illusion that it could be rendered anywhere near *completely* immune.) In his attempts to find out what made men fight he resorted to two different methods. One was to make detailed studies of ancient warfare when battles had been 'simple and clear' and sources, in the form of Polybios, impeccable. The other was a questionnaire which he sent out to his fellow officers and in which he interviewed them very closely about the way their men behaved in combat and the factors which influenced them. In the event, the Franco-Prussian war broke out and du Picq himself was killed before he had received many answers. Not that it mattered, for by that time much of his *Études de combat* (Battle Studies) was largely complete and his mind had been made up.

Fighting against non-European peoples, du Picq had been able to witness the power of military organization at first hand – had not Napoleon said that whereas one Mameluk was the equal of three Frenchmen, one hundred Frenchmen could confidently take on five times their number in Mameluks? Individually men were often cowards; having trained together and standing together in formation, however, they became transformed. A new social force,

known as cohesion, made its appearance as comrade sustained comrade and mutual shame prevented each one from running away. To paraphrase: four men who do not know each other will hesitate to confront a lion; but once they know each other and feel they can trust one another they will do so without fear. *That*, rather than any clever evolutions which it might carry out, was the secret of the ancient Greek and Macedonian phalanx in which men, packed closely together in their ranks and files, sustained each other and, if necessary, physically pushed each other into battle while preventing any escape. The phalanx was, however, if anything too closely packed, with the result that those in front had no way to break away and rest from their ordeal whereas those in the rear were almost as exposed to the fury of battle as their comrades in front. Much better was the chequerboard formation of the Roman legion. Made up of carefully placed smaller units and arrayed in three successive lines (*acies*), it enjoyed all the advantages of the phalanx while still enabling the majority of combatants to catch their breath and recuperate between bouts of fighting.

Now to the really decisive question: how to ensure that men did not break in front of the five rounds per minute which could be directed at them by contemporary weapons? Du Picq's answer is that greater reliance should be placed upon skirmishers, and that 'every officer should be reduced who does not utilize them to some degree'. Skirmishers, however, should be closely controlled; there is no point in sending them so far ahead that, feeling isolated, they will merely hide or run. Controlling the skirmishers is the job of the battalion

During the American Civil War (1861–5), the commanders on both sides are said to have taken the field with copies of Jomini in their pockets. The picture shows how General Sherman 'made Georgia howl'.

commander (since the battalion is the largest unit whose commander can still be in direct touch with the rank and file during battle, du Picq tends to disregard the activities of more senior officers). To enable him to do so, the size of the battalions ought to be cut down by a third, from six to four companies. As one battalion engages in skirmishing, another should be left standing close by, sustaining its sister in the manner of the Roman maniples. Accordingly, the contemporary view of gaps in the line as dangerous is mistaken; on the contrary, and still in the manner of the Roman maniples, such gaps should be deliberately used in order to enable some battalions to advance towards the enemy and the remainder to rest. Care should be taken that the supporting troops belong to the

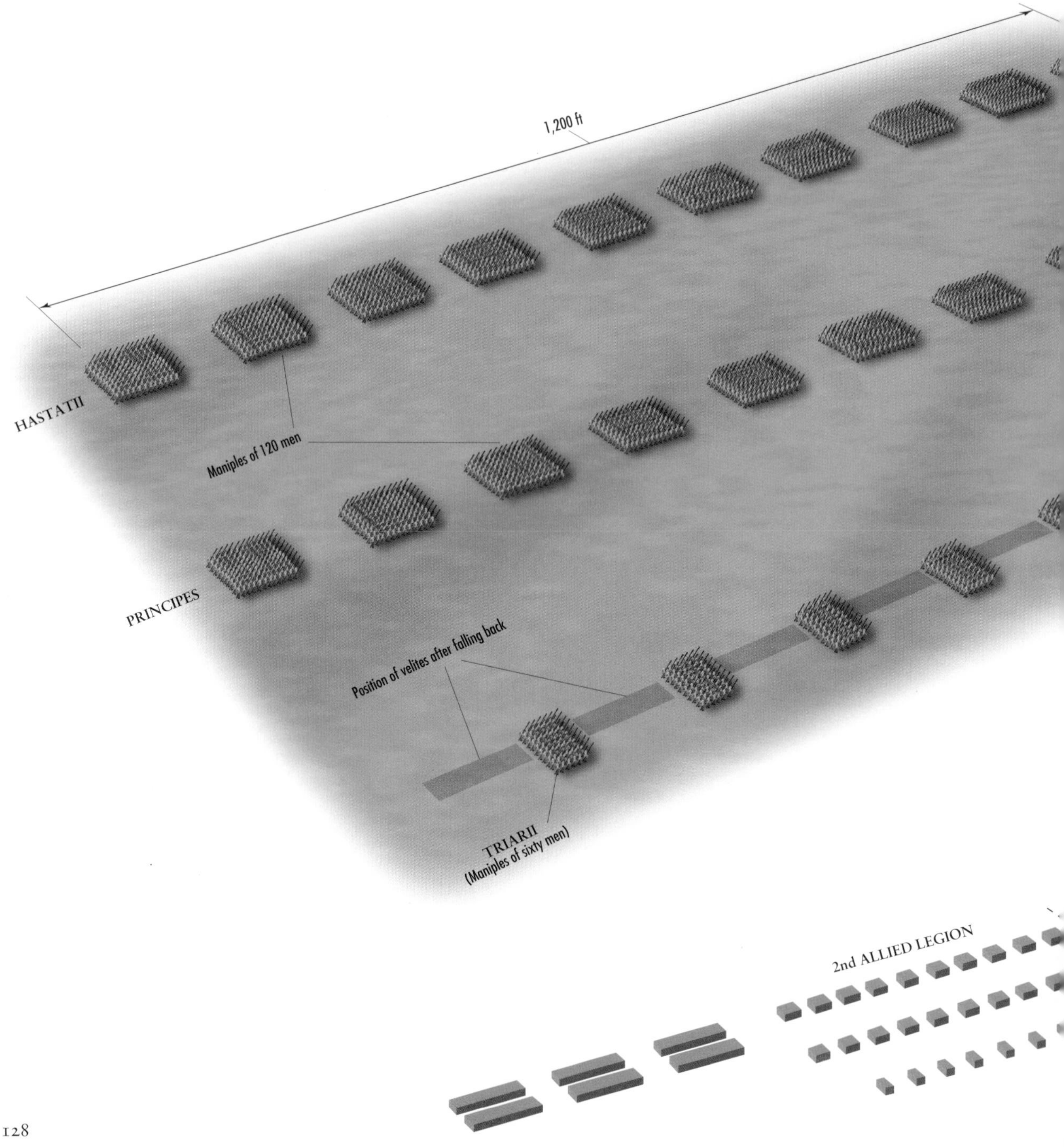

1,200 ft

HASTATI

Maniples of 120 men

PRINCIPES

Position of velites after falling back

TRIARII
(Maniples of sixty men)

2nd ALLIED LEGION

same units as the skirmishers, and vice versa. Any attempt to make troops fire on command should be discouraged.

During his lifetime the work of du Picq, whose professional career was anything but extraordinary, drew little attention. This, however, changed during the late 1890s when the French, having recovered from the defeat of 1870–71, began looking for a method by which they might one day attack and defeat the superior German army so as to regain Alsace–Lorraine. *Battle Studies* was disinterred, and its author turned into the patron saint of the *furor Galicus* school of warfighting. Good organization, unit cohesion, thorough training, firm command, patriotism and the alleged native qualities of the French soldier were

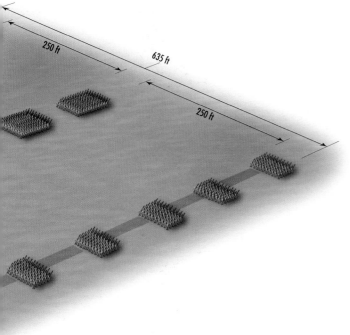

A ROMAN LEGION DEPLOYED FOR BATTLE, THIRD–SECOND CENTURY BC

The main strength of the Roman legion was the heavy infantry, divided into three lines according to age and experience. The youngest (hastati) formed the front line, the more mature men (principes) the second, and the veterans (triarii) were in the rear. Each line was divided into ten maniples, each led by two centurions. The maniples of the three lines deployed in a chequerboard (quincunx) formation, staggered so that they covered the intervals in the line in front. This allowed the reserve lines to be fed into the fighting line to reinforce an attack or, if things went badly, the forward lines to retreat behind the men to their rear. Light infantry (velites) operated in front of the main line, withdrawing through the intervals when pressed.

250 ft

635 ft

250 ft

2d ROMAN LEGION

1st ROMAN LEGION

1st ALLIED LEGION

*The Union Commander
General William T. Sherman
during the American Civil
War.*

to turn him into an irresistible fighting animal – had not Ammianus Marcellinus in the fourth century AD described his ancestors as 'tall of stature, fair and ruddy, terrible for the fierceness of their eyes, fond of quarrelling, and overbearing insolence'? In the autumn of 1914, that approach, complete with the famous *pantalons rouges*, led straight into the muzzles of the waiting German machine-guns. But for this du Picq, who had always emphasized the power of the defence and who had spent much of his professional career worrying lest modern soldiers would *not* be able to confront modern fire, can scarcely be blamed.

Partly because he never rose beyond colonel, partly because his main interest was the heart of man and the factors which enabled it to function in battle, du Picq has very little to say about strategy. To the majority of officers, however, strategy was precisely the key to large-scale war, an esoteric branch of knowledge which they alone possessed and which was intellectually much more satisfying than any mere psychological analysis of the rank and file could ever be. Accordingly, throughout the first half of the nineteenth century the most important military theoretician by far was considered to be Jomini; and, indeed, if the rumour that generals in the American Civil War carried him in their pockets may be exaggerated, there is no doubt that his influence can be discerned for example in the Antietam and Chancellorsville campaigns, as well as in Sherman's march through Georgia to South Carolina. What was more, just as the new rapid-firing arms began to transform combat from about 1830, strategy was being revolutionized by the introduction of railways. Hitherto lines of communication had been somewhat nebulous concepts; now they were reconstructed in a new, cast-iron form which anyone could trace on the ground or on a map. Clearly here was a novel instrument which had to be mastered if it was to be successfully harnessed to war and conquest.

This is not the place to outline the impact of railways on strategy and logistics, a topic that has been the subject of several excellent monographs. Suffice it to say that, outside the US (which, however, produced no military theoretical writings of any importance), nobody was more closely associated with their use for war and conquest than the Prussian chief of staff, Helmut von Moltke. Born in 1800, rising to prominence through sheer intellectual qualities

THE BREECH-LOADING REPEATER RIFLE

The advent of the breech-loading repeating rifle enabled the soldier to fire more aimed shots than the previous muzzle-loading single-shot weapon. The weapon could also be fired from a concealed position, which influenced battlefield tactics from the 1860s onwards.

rather than by way of practical experience (he never commanded any unit larger than a battalion), Moltke, though he possessed a well-educated pen, never wrote a single definitive work. Instead his thought must be garnered from the campaigns he conducted so successfully and, to an equal extent, the series of great memoranda which, in his capacity as chief of General Staff, he wrote between about 1857 and 1873. At heart a practitioner rather than theoretician, Moltke did not bother to go into first principles nor does he mention any of his predecessors. But his memoranda do form a unified coherent whole, which justifies his inclusion in the present study.

To simplify, Moltke's starting point was the rise in the size of armies that had taken place as a result of growing population and industrialization. Instead of

William the Conqueror was one of the most powerful medieval princes, yet at the Battle of Hastings (above) he was only able to muster about 6,500. From his time on the size of armies grew and grew, until by the end of the eighteenth century the largest countries could mobilize hundreds of thousands of men.

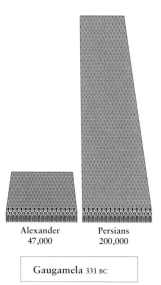

Alexander	Persians
47,000	200,000

Gaugamela 331 BC

Normans	English
6,500	7,000

Hastings 1066

French	Austrians
500,000	450,000

French and Austrian mobilization *c.* 1805

SIZE OF ARMIES

Between the battle of Hastings (left) and the American Civil War (below) the size of armed forces grew by about two orders of magnitude. During the twentieth century the growth continued, climaxing in the Second World War as the largest conflict of all.

During the nineteenth century, assisted by technological developments such as railways and telegraphs, the size of armies continued to grow. During the American Civil War (above), 2 million men passed through the Union Army alone. By the end of the Second World War, the total number of persons in uniform (including approximately 1.5 million women) stood at between 35 and 40 million.

Union
900,000

Confederate
600,000

Union and Confederate
mobilization 1863

Germany
9,000,000

USSR
15,000,000

Second World War 1943–4

OPPOSITE: The introduction of railways revolutionized strategy. Here, French troops are seen entraining, late nineteenth century.

During the nineteenth century the General Staff became the repository of military wisdom. This picture, c. 1890, shows graduates of the French Ecole polytechnique on their way to positions in that august institution.

tens of thousands, they now numbered hundreds of thousands; even a single corps, comprising some 30,000 men, was so large that its sub-units would take an entire day to pass a single point – with the result that the trains making up the rear would be unable to catch up with the front. Prussia, moreover, was the smallest of the five leading European powers. To compensate, alone among those powers it had retained universal conscription (the others either relied on volunteers or adopted some kind of selective service system). Having spent two, later three, years under the colours the conscripts were sent home but remained on call in case of an emergency. The problem was how to mobilize them quickly and deploy them on the frontier, and it was here that the railways came in handy.

Having been appointed chief of General Staff – at a time when that institution was merely a department inside the War Ministry responsible for training, preparation and armament – Moltke went to work. Extremely detailed plans were drawn up for using the railways in order to carry out mobilization and deployment; rehearsed in 1859 and 1864, in 1866 they took the world's breath away as the Prussian army mobilized with an efficiency and at a speed which had previously been considered unattainable. What was more, and as Moltke had expressly foreseen, attaining maximum speed in mobilization meant that as many railways as possible had to be utilized simultaneously. Together with the sheer size of the forces ('a concentrated army is a calamity: it cannot subsist, it cannot

move, it can only fight'), this meant that the troops would be strung out along much of the frontier. A strategy of interior lines of the kind that had been recommended by Jomini and regarded as perhaps *the* single most important device of all would thereby become impossible.

To Moltke, therefore, strategy remained what it had been from Buelow onwards: a question of moving large forces about in two-dimensional space so as to put them in the most favourable position for combat (as well as making use of the outcome of combat after it had taken place). Like du Picq, however, he realized that the rise of quick-firing weapons had caused the balance between offence and defence to change. To attack frontally in the face of rifles sighted to 1,200 yards (1,100 metres) and capable of accurately firing six rounds a minute (such as the French chassepots) was suicide; much better look for the enemy's flank and envelop him. Thus the deployment in width, which others regarded as madness when it was carried out against Austria in 1866, was turned into a virtue. (Marx's companion Friedrich Engels, considered a noted military critic at the time, even wrote that the Prussian deployment could only be explained by the fact that the king personally was in command, members of royal families being notoriously feeble-minded.) The enemy would be caught between armies coming from two, possibly three, directions, and be crushed between them – 'the highest feat which strategy can achieve', to quote a letter which Moltke wrote to the historian Heinrich von Treitschke in 1873. Thus, strategically speaking, Moltke intended his armies to take the offensive. Tactically the troops were supposed to make use of their firepower and remain on the defensive, although in practice that order was not always obeyed.

Marx's friend Friedrich Engels specialized in military history. Some of his articles, published anonymously, were considered good enough to have come from the pen of 'a Prussian general'.

To carry out the mobilization and co-ordinate the moves of his widely dispersed forces Moltke made use of another new technical instrument, the telegraph. The railways themselves could only be operated to maximum effect if the trains' movements were carefully co-ordinated, therefore wires and tracks tended to run in parallel. This enabled Moltke to implement his strategy of external lines *and* remain in control, previously an unheard-of feat. The contemporary telegraph was, however, a slow instrument; with encryption and decryption procedures necessary at both ends (wire-tapping had been practised both during the American Civil War and in the Austrian–Prussian War), the pace at which it could transmit messages became even slower. Again turning necessity into a virtue – the mark of a truly great general – Moltke

French chassepot.

devised his system of directives or *Weisungen*, insisting that orders be short and should only tell subordinate commanders *what* to do, but not how. The system presupposed very good acquaintance and strong mutual trust between officers and thus was possible only thanks to that élite institution, the General Staff, which had its representatives in every major unit. In time it spread from the top down, until in 1936 the volume known as *Truppenführung* (Commanding Troops) announced that 'war demands the free *independent* commitment of every soldier from the private to the general'. The result was a uniquely flexible, yet cohesive, war machine that was the envy of the world.

As already mentioned, unlike many of his eighteenth- and nineteenth-century

A Prussian outpost, 1866.

predecessors, Moltke never produced a 'system' and, indeed, went on record as saying that strategy itself was but a 'system of expedients'. War has a penchant for turning the victor into a fool, however, and post-1871 Imperial Germany was no exception. As Moltke himself noted during his later years – he was to remain in office until 1888, when he could barely any longer mount a horse – the younger generation at the General Staff did not possess their predecessors' broad vision; instead, possibly because of the attention they paid to the railways (an instrument regarded as the key to victory and requiring painstaking attention to detail), they tended to be technically inclined and narrow-minded. Nobody exemplified these tendencies more than the next writer with whom we must concern ourselves here, Alfred von Schlieffen. Born in 1833, in 1891 he was appointed chief of General Staff – by that time, no longer an obscure department in the *Kriegsministerium* but the most prestigious single institution in Germany, with overall responsibility for preparing the land army and leading it into war.

From 1893, the year in which Germany and Russia concluded an alliance, Schlieffen's problem was to prepare his country for war on two fronts. Considering that Germany as the smaller power could not afford to remain on the defensive (as noted earlier, this led to a debate concerning the respective virtues of annihilation versus attrition), the question was, against which one of the two enemies to concentrate first? Schlieffen decided on France, suggesting that its capacity for rapid mobilization made it into the more dangerous enemy and also that geographical circumstances – compared with Russia, France was small – would permit the delivery of a rapid knock-out blow. Like his late nineteenth-century contemporaries, however, Schlieffen was well aware that advancing technology – by now including barbed wire, mines, machine-guns, and cannon provided with recoil mechanisms – favoured the defence. Furthermore, the French border had been fortified. Hence he decided that an outflanking movement was needed and, after considering a left hook and a right one, finally settled on an advance through Belgium.

Having ruminated on all this for years, and prepared the great Plan which will be forever associated with his name, on 1 January 1906 Schlieffen stepped down from his post. He then produced his theoretical masterpiece, a three-page article entitled 'Cannae' after the battle fought by Hannibal against the Romans in 216 BC. From this as well as other essays (particularly 'The Warlord' and 'War in the Modern Age'), it is possible to form an idea of the way in which he, as the person in charge of the most powerful and most sophisticated military machine the world had ever seen, understood war. Tactics and logistics apart (he never showed much interest in either of them), war was the clash of large armies (he never showed any interest in navies) manoeuvring against each other in two-dimensional space. The objective of this manoeuvring was to annihilate (*vernichten*) the other side with the greatest possible dispatch; anything else, though perhaps admissible under particular circumstances, was considered to be a lesser achievement. Now in order to annihilate the enemy it was not enough simply to push him back by applying pressure to his front; given the superior power, under modern conditions, of both the tactical and the strategic defence, such

During the Franco-Prussian War Paris became a bone of contention between the Prussian Chancellor, Otto von Bismarck, and the Army chief of staff, General Helmut von Moltke. Bismarck wanted to capture the city quickly in order to end the war before Austria intervened; Moltke, unwilling to incur casualties, wanted to wait until he could bring up his heavy artillery. The dispute served to illustrate Clausewitz's claim that war is, or ought to be, the continuation of politics.

a procedure would merely result in an 'ordinary' victory after which the enemy, though forced to retreat, would be able to reorganize and renew the struggle. The trick, therefore, was to hold the enemy in front while taking him on the flank, driving him off his lines of communications and, ideally, forcing him to surrender as Moltke for example had succeeded in doing at Sedan in 1870. To Schlieffen's credit, it should be said that he did not believe it was simply a question of geometry. Since an alert enemy would not allow himself to be outflanked easily, he had to be *enticed* into making the wrong moves. 'For a great victory to be won the two opposing commanders must co-operate, each one in his way [*auf seiner Art*].' To a critic who once told him that the art of war was at bottom a simple one, he responded: 'Yes, all it turns on is this stupid question of winning.'

With Schlieffen, we have arrived at the end of the 'long' nineteenth century. It started auspiciously enough with Buelow and Berenhorst presenting their opposing interpretations of the factors which made for victory. Very soon afterwards Jomini and Clausewitz, each in his own way, rid themselves of 'the

According to Helmut von Moltke, encirclement was 'the highest that strategy could achieve'. At the battle of Sedan, 1870, that aim was achieved, leading to the surrender of the French emperor and his army.

ancients' and tried to penetrate the secret of Napoleonic warfare. (Napoleon himself only left behind a list of 'maxims' which, though interesting, do not amount to military theory.) Philosopher that he was, Clausewitz also sought to go much deeper and uncover the fundamentals of warfare by asking what it was and what it served for. To Jomini, the secret was to be found in sophisticated manoeuvring in accordance with a small number of fairly well-defined, geometrically based, principles. Less interested in either geometry or manoeuvring, Clausewitz, before he started revising his work in 1827, put a much greater emphasis on the use of overwhelming force in order to smash the enemy's main forces, after which the rest would be quite easy. Until about 1870, although Clausewitz's greatness was admitted and admired, Jomini was probably the more influential of the two. Then, after the victorious Moltke had pointed to Clausewitz as the greatest single influence on him, the wind shifted. Jomini was studied less, Clausewitz more, often. This was true not only in Germany but in France, where the military revival which started in the 1890s adopted him (in

'German officers fell into two types, the wasp-waisted and the bull-necked' (Barbara Tuchmann). Schlieffen belonged to the former.

addition to du Picq) in order to justify its emphasis on moral forces and its doctrine of the offensive at all costs. Whether or not these doctrines presented the 'true' Clausewitz has often been debated. It is a question to which we shall return.

Meanwhile, it is probably correct to say that Jomini's name was being overlooked not because he was outdated but, on the contrary, because like Lipsius before him he had become so successful that his ideas were being taken very much for granted. Both Moltke and Schlieffen were, in one sense, his disciples, employing his terminology but doing no more than adapting it to their purposes. The former's most important contributions were to make the switch from internal to external lines and to adapt the Swiss writer's doctrines to the new

THE SCHLIEFFEN PLAN 1914

The Schlieffen Plan was the logical result of forty years of development. In it, the Germans tried to realize the idea of encirclement which Schlieffen's predecessor, Helmut von Moltke the Elder, had described as the highest that strategy can aspire to.

technologies represented by the railway and the telegraph; in fact it was precisely the new technologies that forced him to make the switch. Schlieffen was even less original. All he did was present a much simplified, uni-dimensional version of Jomini's thought, limiting it to enveloping operations and combining it with what, rightly or not, he saw as Clausewitz's unrelenting emphasis on the need for a single, climactic, annihilating battle. Nor, as we shall see, did Jomini's career end in 1914. And in fact it could be argued that, as long as large armies go to war against each other in two-dimensional space, making use of communications of every sort, and manoeuvring among all kinds of natural and artificial obstacles, it is his work that will continue to provide the best guide of all.

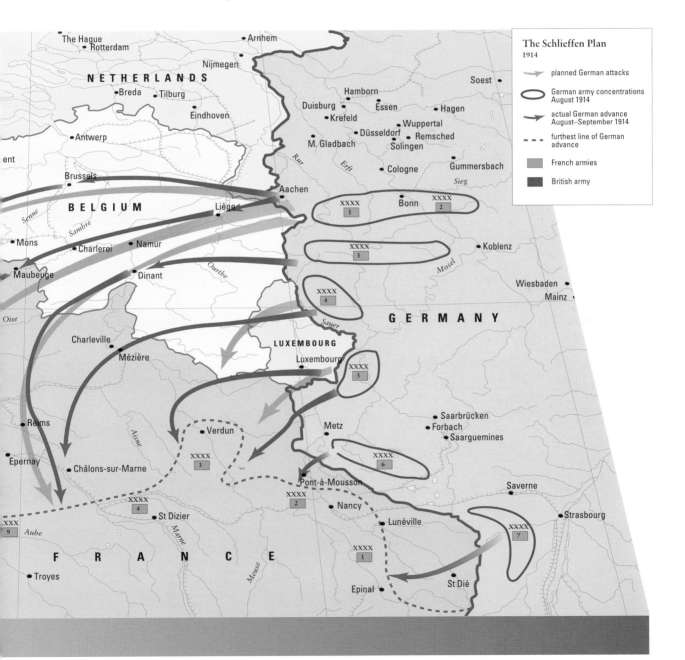

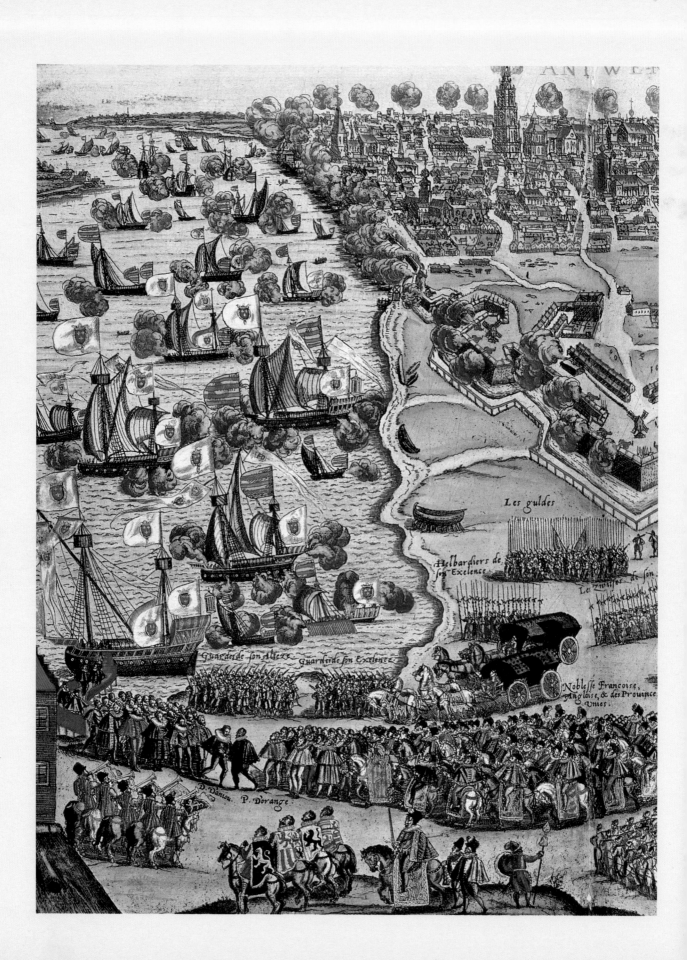

ANTW[...]

Les guldes

Helbardiers de
son Exelence

Les muses de son

Guardes de son Altesse   Guardie de son Excelence

Noblesse Françoise,
Anglaise, & des Provinces
Unies.

D. Daniou. P. Dorange.

CHAPTER SIX

NAVAL WARFARE

*IN THE LATE SIXTEENTH CENTURY Antwerp was the most
important commercial city in Europe. During its siege in
1585, Alexander Farnese, the Duke of Parma, built a
boat-bridge across the River Scheldt in order to cut the city
off from the sea. The besieged sent fire-ships to demolish it,
but ultimately to no avail. The capture of Antwerp on
17 August 1585 by the duke, on behalf of the king of Spain,
Philip II, was an extremely complex enterprise and marked
one of the high points of war during that period.*

NAVAL WARFARE

I N OUR SURVEY so far, naval warfare has barely been mentioned. This is not because the role which it played in war was unimportant; after all, from the Peloponnesian and the Punic wars to those of the Napoleonic era, ships and navies had often figured prominently, sometimes even decisively. Yet even though the ancient Greeks clearly recognized the importance of *thalassocratia* (literally, 'crushing victory at sea'), and even though naval warfare had always been a highly complex and highly technical subject, navies were not made the subject of major theoretical treatises. To be sure, several authors either appended chapters on naval warfare to their works or had others do so, as in the case of for example Vegetius and Jomini. With Vegetius the discussion of naval theory comprised a single page about the importance of having a navy always ready; to this were appended eight short chapters on the principles of building ships, navigating them and fighting them. To Jomini ships were merely an aid to the movements of armies, and what he has to say about them is completely unremarkable. As to Sun Tzu and Clausewitz, the greatest writers of all, to judge by their published works one would think they did not even know that such a thing as the sea existed.

In the study of history room must be allowed for accident. The first staff colleges had been founded in Prussia and France from about 1770. Having

Commodore Stephen Luce, founder of the Naval War College at Newport, Rhode Island.

discovered strategy as the most important subject which they could teach, they began to flourish after 1815 (and even more so after 1871) when every important army in the world felt impelled to have a college. Navies, however, remained backward; it was not until 1885 that an American, Commodore Stephen B. Luce, was able to persuade his country's Navy Department to set up a Naval War College at Newport, Rhode Island, but even then keeping it open and functioning constituted an uphill struggle. After two officers had turned down the job, Luce chose a forty-five-year-old naval captain of no great distinction, Alfred Mahan, to act as chief instructor. Besides the fact that he was the son of Dennis Mahan, a well-known professor at West Point, Alfred Mahan had also written a volume called *The Navy in the Civil War, the Gulf and Inland Waters*. With that, though, his qualifications ended.

If a death sentence is said to 'concentrate the mind wonderfully', so – in the case of some people at any rate – does the requirement to stand in front of a class and teach. Mahan taught class from 1886 to 1889 and in 1890 published his lectures in the form of a two-volume work, *The Influence of Seapower upon History, 1660–1783*. It was an immense success, probably selling more copies than all its predecessors on military theory put together (the first edition of Clausewitz comprised only 500 copies) and earning its author fame not only in the US but in Britain and Germany where the kaiser kept it at his bedside and made every naval officer read it. This success in turn was due to the fact that, in an age dominated by several great and would-be great world powers, Mahan had succeeded in putting together a remarkably coherent case as to why such powers should have navies, what having such navies entailed and how they ought to be used.

The book's main theoretical message is contained in the first and last chapters, the remainder serving to illustrate how naval power had been successfully applied by the most important naval country of all, Britain. Its main concern was strategy: convinced that continuing technological progress must soon render the details of building ships, arming them, sailing and fighting them obsolete, Mahan chose not to elaborate on those subjects. Strategy, on the other hand, was concerned with such questions as 'the proper function of the navy in war; its true objective; the point or points upon which it should be concentrated; the establishment of depots of coal and supplies; the maintenance of communications between those depots and the home base; the military value of commerce-destroying as a decisive or secondary operation of war; [and] the system upon which commerce-destroying can be most efficiently conducted'. In common with many other nineteenth-century theorists Mahan believed that it could be reduced to a small number of principles, and concerning those principles history had a great deal to say.

Describing his own intellectual development, Mahan says that he had first been led to reflect upon these questions while reading the account of Theodor Mommsen (1817–1903) of the critical role played by sea-power during the Punic wars. Not having control of the sea, the Carthaginian navy had been reduced to operating mainly in home waters; beyond these it could do no more than mount occasional raids and forays. Specifically, Carthage had been unable either to reinforce Hannibal's Italian campaign – which, in spite of its commander's genius, was thereby doomed to fail – or to help its principal ally in Sicily, Syracuse. Rome, on the other hand, was able to use its command of the sea in

Captain Alfred Mahan was picked by Luce to become chief instructor at the newly founded Naval War College. His book, The Influence of Seapower on History, *was based on the lectures he gave there and became the most famous treatise on the subject ever.*

The works of Theodor
Mommsen, Nobel prize-
winning historian of ancient
Rome, provided the impetus
to Mahan's thought.

LAND VERSUS MARITIME
POWER *c.* 1812

*The French Revolutionary
and Napoleonic Wars were
fought both on land and at
sea. The map shows the
armies and navies of the
two sides as they were
around 1812.*

order to cut Hannibal off from his bases in Africa
and Spain (the overland route from the latter to
Italy by way of the Alps being perilous and, most
of the time, blocked by the Romans), ship its own
legions to both Spain and Sicily unhindered, keep
King Philip V of Macedonia out of the war
(whether this part of Mahan's argument stands up
to scrutiny is doubtful), and finally invade Africa
itself. Thus sea-power had helped shape the
conduct of the war from beginning to end. It had
also played a crucial part in Rome's victory.

In this as in so many subsequent wars, the
importance of the sea was that it served as a great
highway across which could be transported men,
armies and goods more efficiently, and more
cheaply, than could be done on land. In both war
and peace, the side which was able to do so enjoyed
a critical advantage over the one that could not; this was never more so than in the
late nineteenth century, when so much of every advanced nation's wealth had
come to depend on its ability to export its industrial products while importing
food and raw materials to feed its population and keep its factories running.
During wartime, ensuring passage for one's own side while denying it to one's
opponent was the function of the navy. Put in other terms, the navy of a great
power – like almost all nineteenth-century military theorists except for du Picq,
Mahan was interested in none but great powers – found itself confronted by a
double task: a negative one and a positive one. The negative part consisted of
halting and destroying the enemy's commerce, the positive one of making sure
that one's own ships got through to their destinations. In carrying out this double
mission two strategies presented themselves. One was to protect one's own
shipping by providing it with escorts while simultaneously going after the
enemy's cargo-bearing vessels, a strategy known as *guerre de course* and often
resorted to by past belligerents. The other was to build up as powerful a battle-
fleet as possible and use it to seek out and defeat the other side's navy. With
command of the sea thus achieved, protecting one's own commerce while
sweeping the enemy's remaining ships off the sea and blockading them in their
ports would be relatively easy.

In other words, not for Mahan either war on commerce or its converse,
escorted convoys, both of which constituted half-hearted solutions and merely
led to the dispersal of forces. Instead one should seek and achieve command of
the sea, the sea being treated almost as if it were some piece of country capable
of being conquered and ruled over. At this point the similarity between Mahan
and Clausewitz – at least the early Clausewitz, before he started thinking of
limited war – becomes obvious. Though he never mentions the Prussian, our

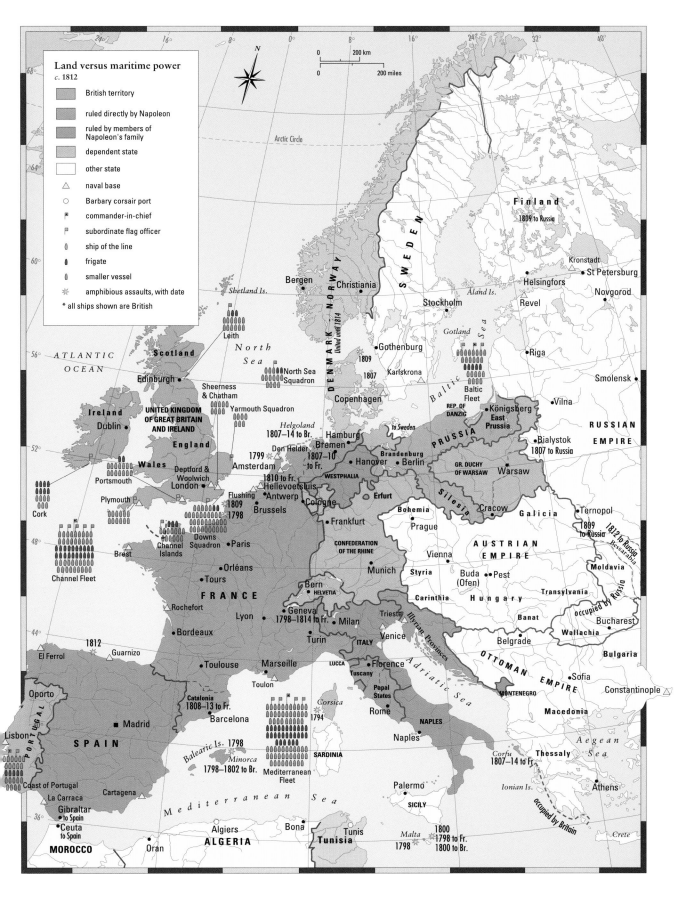

Land versus maritime power
c. 1812

British territory

ruled directly by Napoleon

ruled by members of
Napoleon's family

dependent state

other state

△ naval base

○ Barbary corsair port

⚑ commander-in-chief

⚑ subordinate flag officer

⬗ ship of the line

⬗ frigate

⬗ smaller vessel

✳ amphibious assaults, with date

* all ships shown are British

Arctic Circle

ATLANTIC
OCEAN

Shetland Is.

Bergen

Christiania

North
Sea

Leith

Scotland

Edinburgh

Sheerness
& Chatham

North Sea
Squadron

Ireland

Dublin

UNITED KINGDOM
OF GREAT BRITAIN
AND IRELAND

Yarmouth Squadron

Helgoland
1807–14 to Br.

Wales

England

Deptford &
Woolwich

London

Den Helder

Amsterdam

1799

Portsmouth

Plymouth

Channel
Islands

Flushing
1809
1798

Hellevoetsluis
1810 to Fr.

Hamburg

Bremen
1807–10
to Fr.

Hanover

to Sweden

Cork

Brest

Channel Fleet

Downs
Squadron

Paris

Orléans

Tours

FRANCE

Rochefort

Lyon

Bordeaux

1812

El Ferrol

Guarnizo

Toulouse

Oporto

Madrid

SPAIN

Catalonia
1808–13 to Fr.

Barcelona

Balearic Is. 1798

Minorca
1798–1802 to Br.

Mediterranean
Fleet

SARDINIA

Lisbon

PORTUGAL

Coast of Portugal

La Carraca

Cartagena

Gibraltar
to Spain

Ceuta
to Spain

MOROCCO

Oran

Algiers

ALGERIA

Bona

Mediterranean Sea

Tunis

TUNISIA

Corsica

1794

Antwerp

Cologne

Brussels

Frankfurt

WESTPHALIA

Erfurt

CONFEDERATION
OF THE RHINE

Bern

HELVETIA

Geneva
1798–1814 to Fr.

Milan

Turin

ITALY

Marseille

LUCCA

Toulouse

Toulon

Tuscany

Florence

Papal
States

Rome

NAPLES

Naples

Palermo

SICILY

Munich

Vienna

Styria

Carinthia

AUSTRIAN
EMPIRE

Buda
(Ofen)

Pest

Hungary

Trieste

Venice

Adriatic Sea

Illyrian Provinces

Bohemia

Prague

Silesia

Cracow

Galicia

Ternopol

1809
to Russia

1812 to Russia

Bessarabia

Moldavia

Transylvania

Banat

Wallachia

Belgrade

OTTOMAN EMPIRE

Bulgaria

Sofia

Bucharest

occupied by Russia

Montenegro

Macedonia

Constantinople

*Aegean
Sea*

Thessaly

Corfu
1807–14 to Fr.

Ionian Is.

Athens

occupied by Britain

Crete

Malta
1798 to Fr.
1800 to Br.

1798

1800

DENMARK
United until 1814

NORWAY

SWEDEN

Stockholm

Gothenburg

1809

1807

Copenhagen

Karlskrona

*Baltic
Sea*

Gotland

REP. OF
DANZIG

PRUSSIA

Baltic
Fleet

Königsberg
East
Prussia

Brandenburg

Berlin

Hanover

GR. DUCHY
OF WARSAW

Warsaw

Bialystok
1807 to Russia

1809
to Russia

Åland Is.

Finland
1809 to Russia

Helsingfors

Revel

Kronstadt

St Petersburg

Novgorod

Riga

Vilna

Smolensk

RUSSIAN
EMPIRE

American born-and-bred prophet of sea-power might have said that the best naval strategy was always to be very strong, first in general and then at the decisive point. Once created, the battle-fleet should be kept as concentrated as circumstances permitted and launched straight at the opposing fleet with the objective of annihilating it. Thus considered, Mahan's work represents one long diatribe against commerce-raiding (as well as the minor vessels by which, on the whole, it is carried out) and in favour of navies made up of the most powerful capital ships which can be built. Needless to say, this also entailed massive investments in other components of naval infrastructure such as qualified manpower, ports, depots, dry docks, shipyards, plant for manufacturing arms and armour, and communications like the Suez Canal, the Panama Canal and the Kiel Canal. All of this Mahan explains at some length, which in turn contributed to his popularity not only in naval circles but among certain segments of industry and the political world as well.

As Mahan saw things, sea-power required not merely ships but an extensive naval infrastructure as well; Britain's Chatham Docks, c. 1860.

As already mentioned, in setting forth his views Mahan had drawn mainly on what he interpreted as the historical experience of the strongest modern naval power of all, Britain. Always tending to be pragmatic, though, the British had never been among the great producers of military theory, naval theory included. It was only a decade and a half after Luce had opened the US Naval War College that a similar reform could be carried through the British navy; and even then many officers continued to argue that, especially in view of the navy's past record, a theoretical education was not really needed. It is therefore not surprising that the next important naval author whom we must consider here, Julian Corbett (1854–1922), had much to say concerning the importance of theory as such. To him, it was 'a process by which we co-ordinate our ideas, define the meaning of the words we use, grasp the difference between essential and unessential factors, and fix and expose the fundamental data on which every one is agreed. In this way we prepare the apparatus of practical discussion … Without such an apparatus no two men can even think on the same line; much less can they ever hope to detach the real point of difference that divides them and isolate it for

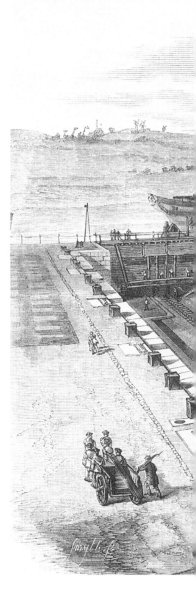

quiet solution'. Achieving common ground was all the more true in the case of an empire such as the British one whose strategy would be made not by a single person or group at a single place but in innumerable conferences held at different places all around the world.

To be taught their own trade by a civilian – by training Corbett was a lawyer, but being a man of independent means he did not practise his profession and wrote full-time – was regarded by many naval officers as an affront. (As one officer wrote, Corbett had 'permitted himself the indulgence of offering his audience his own views on the correctness or otherwise of the strategy adopted by naval officers in the past. His audience had usually treated his amateur excursions into the subject good-naturedly; nevertheless his presumption has been resented, and he has apparently been deaf to the polite hints thrown out to

OVERLEAF: *Both Mahan and Corbett considered communications to be an essential element in naval power. This shows the Suez Canal as it was in 1864.*

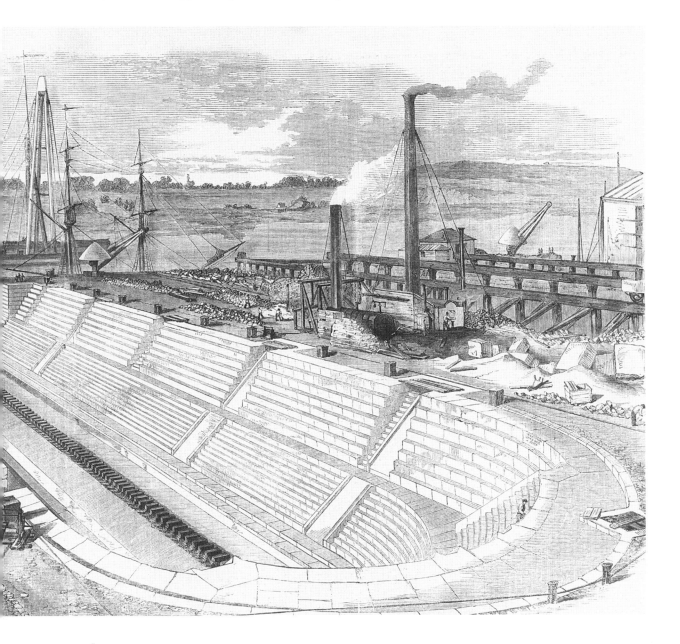

him'.) Had they been able to foresee the contents of his most important theoretical work, *Some Principles of Maritime Strategy*, which came out in 1911, no doubt they would have been doubly offended. If only because he had no true forerunners, Mahan's heroes were figures such as Colbert (who, working for Louis XIV, had created the modern French navy) and Nelson (who more than anybody else had implemented the strategy of the decisive battle). By contrast, Corbett followed good, approved late nineteenth-century practice in that he harnessed Clausewitz and Jomini to his cause. From the former he took the idea that naval warfare, like war as a whole, was merely a continuation of politics by other means. Jomini, Clausewitz's 'great contemporary and rival', was said to have 'entirely endorsed this view'.

Having thus pulled naval warfare down a peg – focusing on the fleet, Mahan had written almost as if policy did not exist – Corbett proceeded to explain that, on the whole, the fact that 'men live upon land and not upon the sea' meant that warfare on the latter was less important, and less decisive, than on the former. History could count many wars which had been decided purely on land without any reference to operations at sea. The reverse, however, was not true; and indeed this even applied to the second Punic war, which Mahan had used as his starting point and case-study *par excellence*. In their more mature days, both Clausewitz and Jomini had concluded that offensive war *à outrance* was only one form of war and that policy might dictate the use of other, more circumscribed methods;

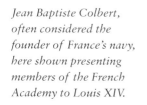

Jean Baptiste Colbert, often considered the founder of France's navy, here shown presenting members of the French Academy to Louis XIV.

the latter had also shown, in considerable detail, how manoeuvres by widely dispersed forces could lead to interesting strategic combinations and result in victory. Add the fact that at sea as on land the defensive was the more powerful form of war, and Mahan's prescription for using the concentrated fleet for seeking out the enemy and dealing a single offensive blow turned out to be completely wrong. Instead, and other things being equal, a compelling case could be made in favour of a careful, and necessarily prolonged, struggle of attrition – safeguarding one's own commerce, disrupting that of the enemy by every means that came to hand, and using the navy to land forces at selected points in the enemy's rear so as to disrupt his plans and throw him out of gear. All this was particularly true if the political entity waging the war was not a country facing a neighbour but a far-flung empire dependent on its lines of communication.

A much better historian than Mahan, Corbett was able to support his argument by means of detailed case-studies. The most comprehensive of these was *England in the Seven Years War*, published in 1907 specifically in order to refute Mahan and quickly getting into the 'limitations of naval action'. Acting on a grand design thought out by Pitt 'the Elder', most of the time the British had *not* attempted to seek out the main French fleet and bring it to battle. Instead they had striven to contain the enemy and limit his movements; all the while protecting their own commerce and using their superior sea-power to assist their allies and grab prizes (such as India and Quebec) that came their way. The result of this

OVERLEAF: *Mahan's vision realized: America's victorious fleet enters New York harbour following the Spanish–American War, 1898.*

The way Mahan saw it, Admiral Nelson was the greatest practitioner of naval power ever, and decisively proved his own theories concerning the need to sweep the enemy fleet off the seas. The picture shows Nelson explaining his plan of attack prior to the Battle of Trafalgar.

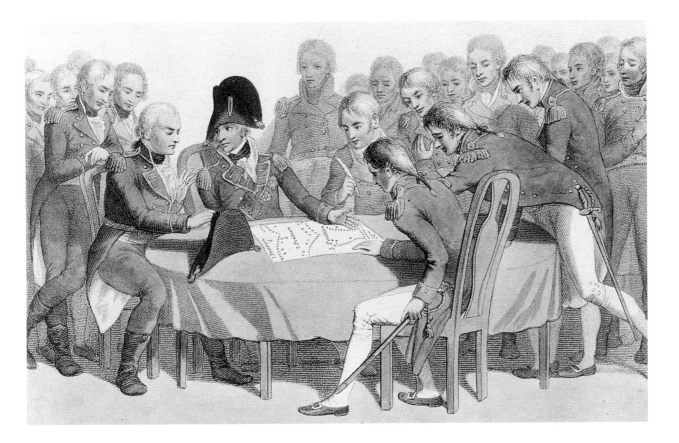

'combined strategy' might not be decisive in the sense aimed at by Mahan. Though many combats took place, no general action between the two fleets was ever fought. When the war ended, not only had the British not achieved complete 'command of the sea' (in so far as French commerce-raiding still continued) but the main French fleet remained in being. Though achieved by strangulation rather than by some smashing victory, the Peace of Paris was 'the most triumphant we ever made'. As such, it marked a critical step on Britain's way to world empire.

Compared to those who came before and after them, Mahan and Corbett were giants. Blunt and to the point, the former can justly claim to have been the first writer who spelled out a comprehensive theory of naval warfare, a subject which hitherto had either been treated as secondary or neglected altogether. Highly sophisticated and tending towards understatement, the latter served as a useful corrective by emphasizing the limitations of maritime strategy and pointing out that command of the sea might be extremely useful even if it was not brought about by a climactic battle between the concentrated fleets of both sides and even if, as a result, it was not as absolute as Mahan would have wished. The unique stature enjoyed by both authors has much to do with the fact that, instead of contenting themselves with the technical aspects of ports, navigation, ships and weapons, they started from first principles. Mahan looked into the objectives of naval warfare *per se*; Corbett linked it to policy, which might be less limited or more so.

Sic transit gloria; a poster entitled 'Naval Heroes of the United States', published in 1864.

With these two approaches to naval warfare in front of them, it would almost be true to say that subsequent theorists were left with little more than crumbs to argue about. As new technological devices such as the submarine and the aircraft joined naval warfare, some believed that Mahan had thereby been rendered obsolete. As two world wars showed, the introduction of submarines made commerce-raiding a much more formidable proposition, whereas aircraft threatened to take command of the sea away from ships, or at least to prevent fleets from approaching close to the land and thus making it much harder for them to force their opponents into battle. The Mahanist response, naturally enough, was to use aircraft in order to combat submarines and put at least some of them on board ships. By doing so they greatly increased the power of the capital ship and the range at which it was able to bring its weapons to bear, and, as Mahan's followers claimed, turned command of the sea into a much more viable proposition than he himself could ever have dreamt of.

As the twentieth century draws to its end both schools are alive and well,

though it must be admitted that the debate has become somewhat academic. Command of the sea in the grand style, implying operations that stretch across entire oceans, is now an objective sought after by one country only; over the last fifty years, even that country has witnessed the number of its aircraft-carriers, as the vital components in that command, dwindle from just under one hundred to a mere twelve. Whether for economic or geographical reasons, virtually all the rest have given up their capital ships and seen their navies reduced to little more than coastguards which are incapable of independent operations far from home. The age of global warfare, which started in the final decades of the seventeenth century (not accidentally, the period in which both Mahan and Corbett open their detailed historical studies), appears to have ended in 1945 and was definitely buried in 1991 when the Soviet Union collapsed, taking the Red navy with it – leaving, one fears *and* hopes, precious little meat for naval theorists to sink their teeth into.

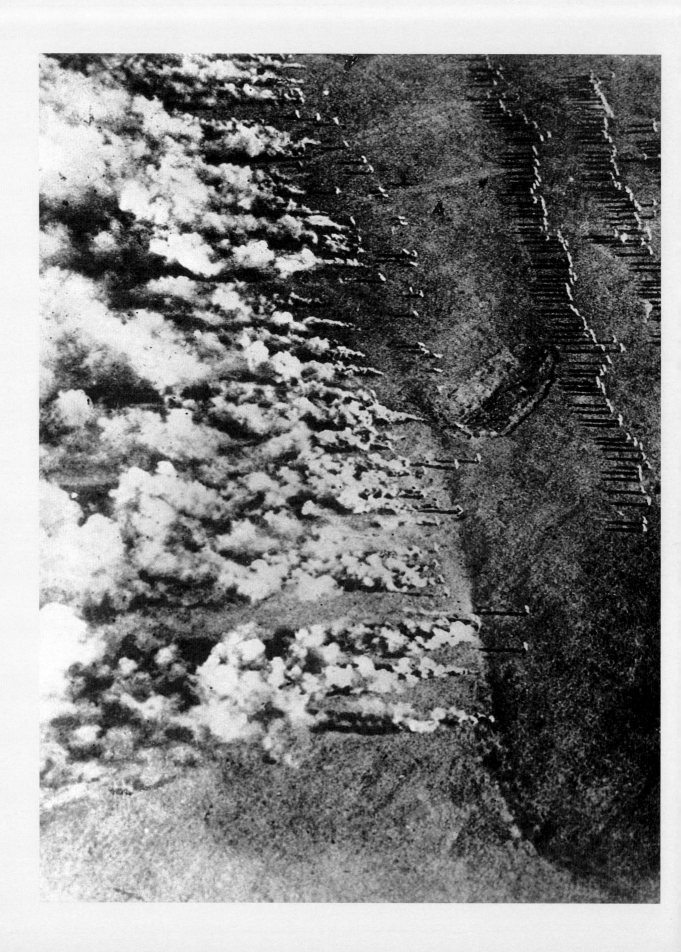

CHAPTER SEVEN

THE INTERWAR PERIOD

GAS BEING RELEASED from its cylinders on the Eastern Front, First World War. Compared to other weapons gas was relatively humane: only a fraction of those exposed to it died. Fighting while wearing protective gear was almost impossible, however, with the result that soldiers hated it, and gas has since been outlawed.

THE INTERWAR PERIOD

THROUGHOUT HISTORY, all too often the conclusion of each armed conflict has served as a prelude to the next one. Never was this more true than at the end of the First World War (known to contemporaries as the Great War) which, although it was sometimes described as 'the war to end all wars', only provided a temporary respite. In fact, scarcely had the guns fallen silent than people started looking into the future on the assumption that the 'great powers' of this world had not yet finished fighting each other. Which gave rise to the question, how was this to be done?

To virtually all of those who tried, the point of departure was the need to minimize casualties. True to its name, the Great War had been fought with greater ferocity, and resulted in more dead and injured, than most of its predecessors put together. Confirming the predictions of some pre-war writers such as the Jewish-Polish banker Ivan Bloch, this was the direct result of the superiority of the defence as brought about by modern fire-power; hence the most pressing problem was to try to find ways to bypass, or overcome, that fire-power and that defence. Failure to do so might render the next war as unprofitable as, in the eyes of many, the struggle of 1914–18 had been, to say nothing of the possibility that the dreadful losses and destruction suffered might cause it to end in revolution, as had already happened in Russia, Austria–Hungary and Germany.

'The Great War' was fought with greater ferocity and resulted in more dead and injured than most of its predecessors put together. Here, German soldiers prepare to bury British dead, 1918.

In the event, the first serious theoretical treatise designed to solve the problem was written by an Italian general, Giulio Douhet. An engineer by trade, during the early years of the century Douhet had become fascinated with the military possibilities of the internal combustion engine. A little later he was also found dabbling in futurist ideas concerning the spiritual qualities allegedly springing from those two speedy new vehicles, the motor car and the aircraft, claiming that they possessed the ability to rejuvenate the world, and Italy in particular. As a staff officer in 1915–18, he was in a position to observe, and reflect on, no fewer than *twelve* Italian offensives directed against the Austrians across the river Isonzo; all failed, producing hundreds of thousands of casualties for little or no territorial gain. Surely there had to be a better way of doing things, one which, in fact, he had already promoted during the war itself, arguing in favour of the creation of a massive bomber force and its use against the enemy. Douhet's masterpiece, *Il Commando del Aereo* (The Command of the Air), was published in 1921. Though it took time to be translated, a survey of the interwar military literature shows that its leading ideas were widely studied and debated.

To Douhet, then, 'the form of any war … depends upon the technical means of war available'. In the past, firearms had revolutionized war; then it was the turn of small-calibre rapid-fire guns, barbed wire and, at sea, the submarine. The most recent additions were the air arm and poison gas, both of them still in their infancy but possessing the potential to 'completely upset all forms of war so far known'. In particular, as long as war was fought only on the surface of the earth, it was necessary for one side to break through the other's defences in order to win. Those defences, however, tended to become stronger

MAXIM, 1908 MODEL, GERMAN

VICKERS, 1912 MODEL, BRITISH

HOTCHKISS, 1914 MODEL, FRENCH

MACHINE-GUNS

The machine-gun was arguably the most important weapon of the First World War. Along with the artillery of the period, it gave the advantage to the defence and thus helped bring about stalemate and trench warfare.

Aircraft offered hope of avoiding scenes such as this one: a French attack repulsed by the Germans at Combres, 1915.

and stronger until, in the conflict that had just ended, they had extended over practically the entire battlefield and barred all troops passage in either direction. Behind the hard crusts presented by the fronts the populations of the various states carried on civilian life almost undisturbed. Mobilizing those populations, the states in question were able to produce what it took to wage total war and sustain the struggle for years on end.

With the advent of the aircraft, this situation was coming to an end. Capable of overflying both fronts and natural obstacles, and possessing a comparatively long range, aircraft would be used to attack civilian centres of population and industry. No effective defence against such attacks was possible; given that the air could be traversed in all directions with equal ease, and that there was no predicting which target would be hit next, to counter each attacking aircraft it would be necessary to have twenty defensive ones or, if the job were entrusted to guns, hundreds if not thousands of them. Extrapolating from the raids that had taken place in 1916–18, Douhet showed that forty aircraft dropping eighty tons of

bombs might have 'completely destroyed' a city the size of Treviso, leaving alive 'very few' of its inhabitants. A mere three aircraft could deliver as much fire-power as could a modern battleship in a single broadside, whereas a thousand aircraft could deliver ten times as much fire-power as could the entire British navy – numbering thirty battleships – in ten broadsides. Yet the price-tag of a single battleship was said to be about equal to that of a thousand aircraft. To use modern terminology, the differential in cost/effectiveness between the two types of arms was little less than phenomenal. As Douhet pointed out, moreover, even these calculations failed to take account of the fact that the career of military aviation had just begun and that aircraft capable of lifting as much as ten tons each might soon be constructed.

Under such circumstances, investments in armies and navies should come to a gradual halt. The resources made free in this way should be diverted to the air arm, regarded as the decisive one in any future conflict and one which, properly used, could bring about a quick decision – so quick, indeed, that there might

An improvised anti-aircraft defence, 1917.

scarcely be sufficient time for the two remaining ones to be mobilized and deployed. Given that the character of the new weapon was inherently offensive, most of the aircraft ought to be not fighters but bombers. Instead of forming part of the army and navy, as was then the case in all major armed forces except those of Britain, they should be assembled in an independent air force. At the outbreak of the next war that air force should be launched like a shell from a cannon, engaging in an all-out attack against the enemy's air bases with the objective of gaining 'command of the air'. Once command of the air had been attained – meaning that the enemy, his bases destroyed, was no longer able to interfere with operations – the attackers should switch from military objectives to civilian ones, knocking them out one by one. Industrial plant as well as

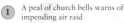

(1) A peal of church bells warns of impending air raid

(2) Fighter escorts defend bombers from possible attack by defending aircraft, including six new Bf 109 fighters of the Condor Legion

(3) Bombers arrive over the city in several waves. Of the twenty-nine bombers attacking the city, twenty-three are Junkers 52/3, shown here

(4) Fighter escorts are also ordered down to low level and attack the town with machine-gun fire

(5) As final waves of bombers complete their mission, the force has dropped some 100,000lbs of bombs, killing approximately 1,000 people and wounding many more

population centres ought to be attacked; the attackers' principal weapon should be gas, the aim not merely to kill but to demoralize. Leaping over and ignoring the usual forces that defend a country, a war waged by such means might be over almost before it had begun. In so far as it would minimize the casualties of both the attacker and the defender (whose population, driven to the point of madness, would force the government to surrender), it also represented a more humane *modus operandi* than an endless struggle of attrition.

Like Mahan, to whom he owed much, Douhet has been accused of overstating his case. When the test came in the Second World War it was found that his calculations, made in terms of a uniform bomb pattern dropping on an area of 500 by 500 metres, had not allowed for the practical difficulties of accurately landing ordnance on target; as a result, far more bombs and aircraft were needed to obliterate a given objective than he had thought. Perhaps because gas was not used, by and large the populations which found themselves at the receiving end of those bombs proved much more resilient than he had expected, causing one critic to quip that Douhet could not be blamed for the fact that the people whom he used as the basis for his calculations were, after all, Italians. (In both world wars, as common wisdom has it, Italians proved themselves to be

OPPOSITE: *The bombardment of Guernica provided an object lesson in what modern air power could do to civilians. This is an anti-Fascist poster by the French artist Pierre Mail.*

DOUHET'S THEORY, GUERNICA

With aircraft such as these, military planners during the interwar period sought to realize Douhet's vision of attaining command of the air and achieving victory by bombarding civilian targets.

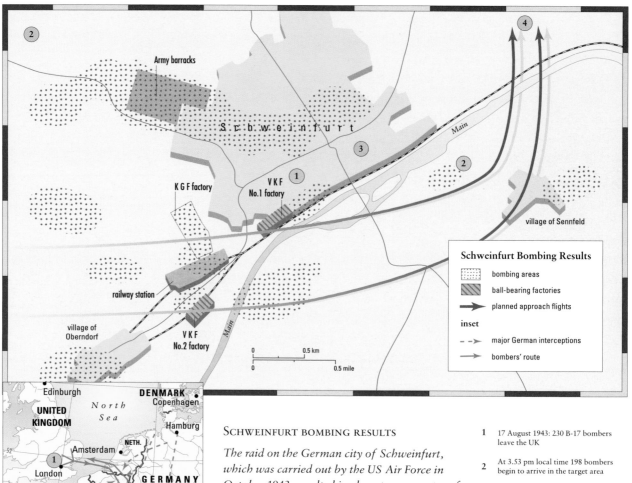

SCHWEINFURT BOMBING RESULTS

The raid on the German city of Schweinfurt, which was carried out by the US Air Force in October 1943, resulted in almost one-quarter of the force being lost. It forced the suspension of the bombing campaign until planners could figure out what to do next.

1   17 August 1943: 230 B-17 bombers leave the UK

2   At 3.53 pm local time 198 bombers begin to arrive in the target area

3   The last bomb falls in the Schweinfurt area at 4.11 pm local time; 184 aircraft release bombs over the target area, dropping 265 tons of high explosive and 115 tons of incendiary

4   Only 194 B-17 bombers return to the UK, of which eighty-one are damaged and have suffered crew casualties. Thirty-six aircraft are lost, together with 361 casualties

1   The warning siren sounds at 3.44 pm. Most people disregard the warning, but eleven batteries of 88mm anti-aircraft guns are manned and ready

2   The raid lasts twelve minutes, with most bombs falling away from the intended targets. Approximately 275 people have been killed in the city and surrounding area. The fighter force attacking the American formations has lost sixteen aircraft

THE PROJECTION OF AIR POWER

Between 1918 and 1945 the ordnance-carrying capacity of the heaviest available bombers increased approximately fivefold. By the latter date 10 tons of ordnance could be carried to a range of 1,500 miles (2,400 kilometres) at approximately 350 miles (560 kilometres) per hour and 30,000 feet (9,000 metres) altitude.

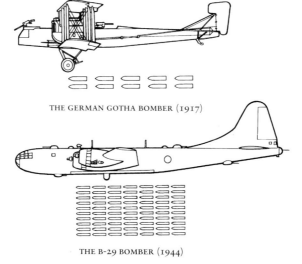

THE GERMAN GOTHA BOMBER (1917)

THE B-29 BOMBER (1944)

Douhet wanted aircraft to attack industrial plants as well as population centres. This shows Woolwich Arsenal, London, in 1918.

Second World War type anti-aircraft radar, 1945.

By the Second World War, anti-aircraft defence looked like this (Salerno, September 1943).

lousy soldiers.) Finally, once radar had been introduced, the air weapon turned out to be much better adapted for defensive purposes than its original prophet – he died in 1930 – had foreseen. In the air, as on land, the Second World War developed into a prolonged and extremely deadly struggle of attrition.

Nevertheless, given that it is with the evolution of military thought that we are dealing here, it should immediately be said that no other treatise written on the subject of air warfare has ever presented nearly as coherent a picture as did *The Command of the Air*, nor has any other treatise ever been as influential. In part, the reasons for this were institutional. Engaging in close air

support (CAS) and interdicting enemy lines of communication were missions which might conceivably be undertaken by an army air force; but gaining command of the air and attacking the opposing side's homeland were clearly independent missions which called for an equally independent air force. Be this as it may, the mirage of dealing a rapid and all-powerful blow from the air – so rapid and so powerful that the need for the remaining armed forces would be all but obviated – continued to fascinate airmen right through the Second World War and into the nuclear age when, but for the fact that nuclear weapons were too destructive to use, it might have been realized.

To carry out the air offensive he envisaged, Douhet had proposed to rely on a comparatively small force made up of élite warriors, a vision which meshed well with the anti-democratic, Fascist ideas that he also entertained. Much the same was true of the great prophet of mechanized warfare on land, the British general John Frederick Fuller. Born nine years after Douhet and destined to outlive him by more than thirty years (he died in 1966), Fuller was a self-taught intellectual whose interests ranged from Greek philosophy to Jewish mysticism or Cabbala. As a young officer before the First World War he had been much concerned to discover the principles of war, finally settling on six. These were: the objective (the true objective was the point at which the enemy may be most decisively defeated), mass, the offensive, security, surprise and movement. From the end of 1916 he found himself acting as chief of staff to the Royal Tank Corps, to whose organization and operations he made a critical contribution.

This is not the place to engage in a detailed examination of Fuller's intellectual development, a task that has been successfully undertaken by several other writers. Suffice it to say that, like so many others, he was appalled by the loss of life which had resulted from trench warfare during the First World War. Like so many others he sought a solution, but unlike so many others he possessed one which had already been tried and applied to some extent. As Bloch had foreseen, the advent of magazine rifles, machine-guns and quick-firing artillery had saturated the battlefield in a storm of steel, making offensive movement practically impossible; what, then, was more natural than to put a

J. F. C. Fuller was chief of staff to the Royal Tank Corps during the First World War and later rose to the rank of major general. Offered to command the experimental armoured force that was being set up during the late 1920s, he refused to do so except on his own terms and resigned from the army.

moving shield in front of the advancing troops? A shield capable of resisting the penetrating power of modern high-velocity bullets and shrapnel was, however, likely to be heavy. Hence it should be provided with an engine and put on wheels or, better still, tracks.

As a serving soldier in France, Fuller was not involved with the early development of the tank, which was the work of others. Later, having gained practical experience in planning armoured forces and operating them, his decisive contribution was to demand, and to suggest ways for, the tank's transformation from a siege-engine – its original purpose – into a modern version of the old heavy cavalry. To put it briefly, crossing trenches and breaking through the enemy's fortified system was one thing, and one which by the end of the First World War was being achieved fairly regularly both by the Germans – who relied on storm-trooper tactics for the purpose – and by the Allies with the assistance of tanks. However, and as was proved *inter alia* by the battle of Cambrai (which Fuller helped plan and direct) in November–December 1917, merely doing so was not enough. To bring about the enemy's collapse it was necessary to push deeper into his territory, attacking his vitals such as command posts, communications and depots, and bringing about his collapse from the rear to the front. Tanks, not the early, cumbersome machines but the more mobile ones that were becoming available towards the end of the war, were to play a vital role in this kind of operation; but so were mobile artillery and aircraft.

Fuller's famous Plan 1919 was intended to realize these ideas but came too late for it to be turned into practice. Once peace had been restored, Fuller, while

The tank's opponent: anti-tank artillery, First World War style.

still in the army, became the principal exponent of mechanization. In numerous publications – he was a prolific writer who, however, often tended to overstate his case – he argued that war, like every other field of human life, was decisively affected by the progress of science. Like Douhet, he considered that currently the most important fruits of science were the internal combustion engine (on which depended the aeroplane and the tank) and poison gas; whether armed forces liked it or not, these devices *had* to be employed because failure to do so was to risk being left behind. Future warfare on land would centre around the tank and be based almost entirely on tracks as artillery, recce units, engineers, signals, supply and maintenance all became mechanized. Once they had mechanized themselves armies would enjoy almost as much freedom of movement as did ships at sea. They would use it in order to manoeuvre against each other, concentrating against select sections of the enemy front, breaking through them and bringing about victory at comparatively low cost.

While not alone in the field, Fuller did as much as anybody to stimulate the debate about tanks and mechanization. Coming as they did from the ex-chief of staff of the most advanced mechanized force in history, his views commanded particular respect. Barring the most extreme ones – for example, the idea that armies should consist of tanks alone and that every infantryman should be provided with his individual tankette and use it to wage guerrilla warfare – many of his suggestions have come to pass; and, indeed, it could be argued that all modern mechanized armies stem from the experimental force which was first assembled on Salisbury Plain in 1928 and of which, had he wished, he could have been the commander. The problem was that, considering himself not merely a reformer but a philosopher, Fuller went on to surround himself with an immensely complicated network of intellectual propositions on the nature of war, life and history. Combining all these different strands, many of his historical writings were decidedly brilliant. However, much of his theorizing was decidedly half-baked: for example, his idea that all things fell 'naturally' into three parts.

In particular, like Douhet, Fuller considered democracy and the mass armies to which it had given rise from the time of the French Revolution to be harmful and degenerate. Also like Douhet, he hoped to replace those mass armies by a small force of élite, tank-riding, professional warriors. Not only would war thereby be conducted much more efficiently, but the example set by such a force would have a regenerating impact on, and serve as a model for, society as a whole. But whereas Douhet was in line with majority opinion in his own country and

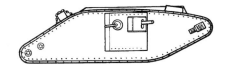

BRITISH FIRST WORLD WAR TANK, MARK I, *c.* 1916–17

BRITISH VICKERS LIGHT TANK, *c.* 1935

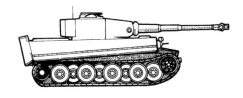

GERMAN TIGER TANK, *c.* 1944

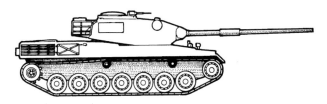

GERMAN LEOPARD TANK, *c.* 1965

THE DEVELOPMENT OF THE TANK

From the time tanks were invented in 1915 to the introduction of the latest generation of battle tanks during the late 1970s these machines underwent several metamorphoses. From the early 1930s, however, no new principles were added and each new tank looked much like a larger version of the previous one.

enjoyed the friendship of Benito Mussolini, Fuller, having resigned from the army in 1928, did himself a lot of harm by joining the British Union of Fascists and writing articles in a Fascist vein. Later he even went to Germany as an official guest of Hitler's in order to attend the Wehrmacht's manoeuvres.

In the history of twentieth-century military thought, Fuller's name is almost always associated with that of his contemporary and friend, Basil Liddell Hart. Born in 1895, unlike Fuller Liddell Hart was not a professional soldier but had studied history at Cambridge for one year before enlisting, receiving a commission and being sent to fight in France. Gassed at the Somme, Captain (throughout his life he enjoyed emphasizing the military rank he had attained) Liddell Hart spent the rest of the war in Britain training volunteer infantry and it was in this capacity that he first started thinking seriously, and writing, about armed conflict. When the war ended, and having been invalided out of the army, he made his living as a sports journalist.

Concerning his intellectual development, two points are worth noting. First, like so many of his generation who, along with him, were educated in public schools, Liddell Hart was brought up on the notion that war was akin to sport and games. In his memoirs he relates, proudly, that he was rather good at

During the 1920s Britain developed the world's most advanced armoured forces. Members of Parliament watching army tank manoeuvres on Salisbury Plain, 1928.

football; not because his co-ordination and technique were in any way outstanding, but because he could engage in various combinations and foresee where the ball was likely to end up. Second, and again like so many of his generation, Liddell Hart ended the war as a fervent admirer of the British military establishment which, after all, had just fought and won the greatest armed conflict in history until then. Within a few years he completely reversed his view, joining the then fashionable trend and becoming disillusioned with the war in general and with its conduct at the hand of the British High Command in particular. In criticizing that conduct, his experience as a popular journalist and interest in games were to come in handy.

Like Fuller, Liddell Hart arrived at the conclusion that sending men to attack frontally in the face of the machine-guns which were trained at them had been the height of folly and only led to masses of unnecessary casualties.

Basil Liddell Hart, as he looked in 1953.

More than Fuller, he took care to trace this folly to its origin which, according to him, was to be found not in simple bloody-mindedness but in the writings of the greatest of all military philosophers, Karl von Clausewitz. As he interpreted Clausewitz – and whether this interpretation is in fact correct has been much debated since – the latter was the 'Mahdi of Mass'; the prophet whose clarion call had misled generations of officers into the belief that the best, indeed almost the only, way to wage war was to form the greatest possible concentration of men and weapons and launch it straight ahead against the enemy. In 1914–18 this 'Prussian Marsellaise' had borne its horrible fruit. The results could be seen on literally thousands of war memorials erected not only in Britain but all over the British Empire and, indeed, the world.

Although, like Fuller, Liddell Hart was largely self-taught, he enjoyed several advantages over the older man. For one thing he was less interested in the non-military aspects of history and philosophy. This caused his historical writings to be somewhat one-dimensional; not for him the scintillating synthesis of politics, economics, sociology and culture that often marks Fuller's work at its best. However, it also saved him from engaging in the kind of mystic flights that sometimes made Fuller appear

LIDDELL HART'S EXPANDING TORRENT

The Expanding Torrent represented Liddell Hart's mature ideas as to how an offensive should be carried out under modern conditions. Combined with tanks and other armoured vehicles, it was the equivalent of the Blitzkrieg. However, in his pre-1939 writings Liddell Hart himself never completed the missing link. Instead, hoping to keep Britain out of another major continental commitment, he went on to explain how, in modern war, the defence was stronger than the offence.

incomprehensible if not unbalanced. He wrote clearly and to the point, and indeed cynics might argue that part of his extraordinary success stemmed from the fact that his work was so simplistic that it could be understood even by generals. By the time he set forth his ideas about Clausewitz in *The Ghost of Napoleon* (originally delivered as the Lees-Knowles lectures for 1933) he was already the most famous military journalist in Britain and, by way of confirming his status, was working for the *Encyclopaedia Britannica* as well. Four years earlier, in 1929, he had set forth his mature doctrines in *The Decisive Wars of History*. Augmented to include the Second World War and reprinted many times under titles such as *Strategy: the Indirect Approach* and *Strategy*, it was to become perhaps the most influential military study of the twentieth century.

Though he started his career as an infantry tactician, much like his predecessors from Jomini onwards, Liddell Hart's main interest was strategy. As with them. this fact caused him to ignore the period from about AD 600 (the wars of Belisarius and Narses) to 1500 (the Franco-Italian wars in Italy), a 900-year period apparently marked by nothing but endless skirmishing in which little of interest took place. For the rest, however, he accepted the late nineteenth-century view, which had been shared by Mahan, Douhet and Fuller, that whereas the forms of war were

Direct attack

subject to change, its fundamental principles were not. (Besides Fuller, the most prominent among those who tried to discover these principles were two Frenchmen, Ferdinand Foch and Jean Colin.) In this way he was able to treat ancient and modern campaigns – beginning with Alexander the Great and ending with Ludendorff in 1918 – as if they were basically similar, ignoring all differences between them and focusing on what, to him, was the essential point. The essential point, arising straight out of the experience of the First World War, was that direct attacks against the enemy's front had to be avoided at all costs since they inevitably ended in failure.

To restore the power of the offensive and save casualties, Liddell Hart went on to recommend 'the indirect approach'. Rather than attacking the enemy head

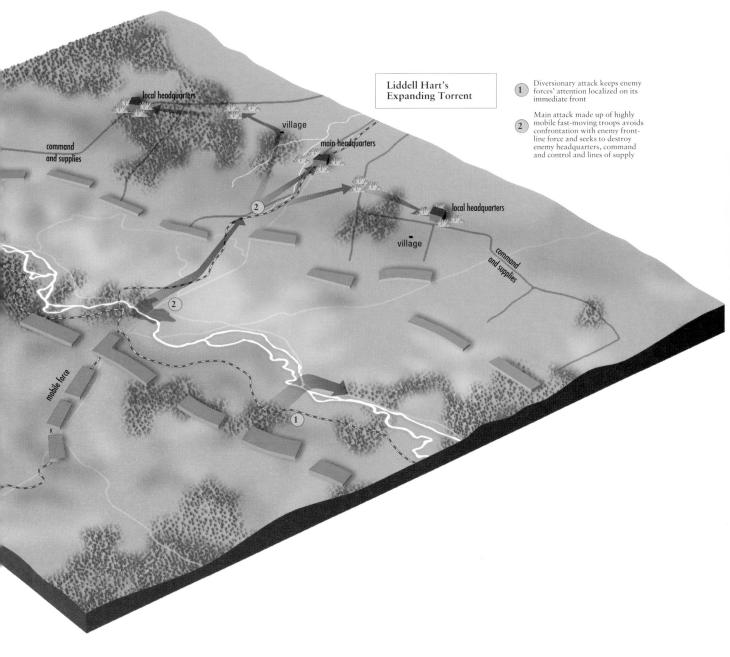

Liddell Hart's Expanding Torrent

1 Diversionary attack keeps enemy forces' attention localized on its immediate front

2 Main attack made up of highly mobile fast-moving troops avoids confrontation with enemy front-line force and seeks to destroy enemy headquarters, command and control and lines of supply

local headquarters

village

main headquarters

command and supplies

local headquarters

village

command and supplies

mobile force

on, he had to be weakened first by having his limbs cut off, his organization disrupted and the mind of his commander unbalanced. As he sought to show at the hand of historical studies – in reality, little more than thumbnail sketches – this could be achieved by combining rapidity of movement with secrecy and surprise, resulting in strokes carried out by dispersed forces (so as to conceal the true centre of gravity for as long as possible), coming from unexpected directions, and following the route of least expectation even if this meant tackling and overcoming topographical obstacles. Above all, every plan had to possess 'two branches', i.e. should be drawn up in such a way as to keep red guessing concerning blue's true objectives. It should also be sufficiently flexible to enable that objective to be changed if, by some mishap, the first one turned out to be too strongly defended.

All these manoeuvres were to be carried out in two-dimensional space, along lines of communication, among all kinds of natural and artificial obstacles, while trailing 'an umbilical cord of supply', and against an enemy who presumably was also capable of manoeuvring. To this extent he owed a lot to Jomini, although it was characteristic of Liddell Hart that, in his *chef-d'oeuvre*, his great predecessor's name is never mentioned. Consisting essentially of movement and characterized by means of coloured arrows stretching across a map, war was presented almost as if it were some kind of sophisticated game played between opposing teams. This was particularly true of his mature work. Having started his career as a trainer of infantry, the older he became, the more pronounced Liddell Hart's tendency to give tactics short shrift. Mobilization, logistics, command, communication and control, and those twin unimportant questions of killing and dying were also lightly skipped over (as he once wrote: 'could one but remove the horrible suffering and mutilation it would be the finest purifier of nations ever known'). Reading his last book, *History of the Second World War* (1970), one might be excused for thinking it was all about operational movement and very little else.

Having once overcome his early admiration for the British performance in the First World War, during the early 1920s Liddell Hart had also become interested in mechanization. In this field his mentor was Fuller, whom he had known since 1920; and indeed so much did the younger man lift – not to say, steal – from the works of the older one that their friendship almost went to the dogs. Liddell Hart's vision of mechanized armed forces was set forth in *Paris, or the Future of War* (1925) as well as *The Remaking of Modern Armies* (1927). In these small but extremely well-written studies he talked about the usual combination of tanks, aircraft and poison gas as weapons with which the defence could be skipped over or overcome, stalemate broken 'within a few hours, or at most days' and the war brought to a swift and cheap, if violent, end.

Given that the main characteristic of both land-based mechanized vehicles and aircraft was speed and flexibility, it might be thought that Liddell Hart should have seized upon them as the ideal tools with which to implement the strategy of indirect approach against opposing, equally mobile, armed forces. Instead, however, he was enticed by a Douhet-like vision of 'London, Manchester, Birmingham and half a dozen other great centres simultaneously attacked, the business localities and Fleet Street wrecked, Whitehall a heap of ruins, the slum districts maddened into the impulse to break loose and maraud, the railways cut, factories destroyed'. As a result, he never quite came around to forging the missing link between the two halves of his vision, the strategic and the technological. Though *Paris* does contain a few brilliant lines on this problem, in *The Decisive Wars of History* the entire question of mechanization is barely mentioned.

What prevented Liddell Hart from making a detailed forecast of the *Blitzkrieg*, with its characteristic combination of armoured divisions and tanks, was his abiding revulsion with the horrors of the First World War and his determination, which he shared with so many of his generation, that they should not be repeated. From about 1931 this caused him to switch from attempts to devise more effective ways to win towards thinking about less costly means to avoid defeat. Following Corbett – once again, without mentioning him by name – he now claimed that the 'British Way in Warfare' had always been to stay out of massive continental commitments. Instead, Britain had relied on its navy to keep the enemy at bay (and harass and weaken him by means of well-directed strokes at selected points), and on continental allies to deliver the *coup de main*. By 1939 he had convinced himself that 'the dominant lesson from the experience of land warfare, for more than a generation past, has been the superiority of the defence over attack'; even in the air, as experiences in Spain had shown, 'the prospects of the defence are improving'. Therefore, instead of Britain repeating its First World War error which had led to so many casualties, it could safely trust the 'dauntless' French to stop the Germans. Britain itself, its armed forces thoroughly modernized and mechanized, should revert to its traditional strategy, relying primarily on blockade on the one hand and air power on the other. This had the additional advantage that it would make universal conscription and mass armies unnecessary – a preference for small professional forces being one thing which Liddell Hart, who unlike Douhet and Fuller was not a Fascist but a liberal, shared with them.

Followed, as they were, by the outstanding success of the early *Blitzkrieg* offensives, these predictions all but discredited Liddell Hart. By the middle of the Second World War he was regarded almost as *passé*; the means, kosher and not so kosher, by which he revived his reputation after 1945 and presented himself as the person who had taught the Germans all they knew need not concern us here. Suffice it to say that all three thinkers discussed in this chapter so far started from the idea that the First World War had provided an example of how *not* to do things. All three were shocked by the number of casualties which had been brought about by the power of the defence. To all three, that power was not the natural result of modern technology (including logistics, a subject to which none of them paid much attention) but, on the contrary, of a failure to make use of its most recent possibilities, whether in the air or on the ground or both. Each in his own way, all three sought to discover ways by which comparatively small but modern armed forces could overcome that defence so as to make it once again possible to wage war quickly and decisively – although, as has just been explained, Liddell Hart ended up by retreating from that proposition.

Compared with Douhet, Fuller and Liddell Hart, Erich Ludendorff was a towering figure. Much more than the former two he understood what modern war was like at the top. Unlike the last-named he did not regard it as some kind of field game – as he wrote, having lost two sons, 'the war has spared me nothing'. On the other hand, and again unlike Liddell Hart in particular, neither did he shrink from its horrors. Ludendorff's post-war dabbling with anti-Semitism, anti-Catholicism and anti-Freemasonry (he could never make up his mind which of the three international forces posed the greatest danger to Germany) bordered on the paranoid and has been rightly condemned. However, this should not be allowed to obscure the fact that his vision of future armed conflict was awesome and, what is more important, more nearly correct than any of the rest.

Having spent over two years in charge of the war effort of the most powerful belligerent in history until then, Ludendorff did not believe that a first-class modern state could be brought to its knees rapidly and cheaply by aircraft dropping bombs on its civilian population. Nor could this be achieved by fleets of tanks engaging in mobile operations, however indirect and however brilliant. In part, Ludendorff merely continued the work of some pre-1914 militarist writers, such as Colmar von der Goltz and Friedrich von Bernhardi, who had advocated total mobilization and mass armies. Up to a point, too, *Der totale Krieg* (the English translation is called *The Nation at War*) both recounted his own experience, and also, by attacking many of his less co-operative colleagues, sought to explain why Germany (with himself at its head) had lost the war. Whatever the book's precise origins and purpose, Ludendorff's main thesis was that the developing technologies of production, transportation and communication made modern war into much more than merely a question of armed forces manoeuvring against each other for mastery of some battlefield. Instead it was 'total' – the title of his book – basing itself on all the forces of the nation, and requiring that the latter be mobilized to the last person and the last screw.

To be sure, the next war would make use of all available modern weapons, including poison gas. Civilians as well as the armed forces would be targeted, and the resulting number of casualties, the destruction and suffering would be immense. Therefore, it would be all the more important to mobilize not only all material resources but also the people's spirit, a point on which, the way Ludendorff and many of his countrymen saw it, Imperial Germany with its old-fashioned, authoritarian system of government and its neglect of the working classes had been sadly deficient. The implication of such mobilization was an end to democracy and the liberties it entailed, including not only freedom of the press but capitalist enterprise as well. For either industrialists or union leaders (during the war Ludendorff had had his troubles with both) to insist on their own privilege was intolerable; they, as well as the entire financial apparatus available to the state, were to be subjected to a military dictatorship. Nor was Ludendorff under any illusion that the nation's spiritual and material mobilization could be quickly improvised. Hence the dictatorship which he demanded, and for which he no doubt regarded himself as the most suitable candidate, was to be set up in peacetime and made permanent.

The next war would not be a gentlemanly fight for limited stakes to be won by the side with the swiftest and sharpest sword. Instead it would be a life and death struggle won by the belligerent with the greatest resources and the strongest will-power – which incidentally disposed of any childish illusions concerning small, professional and highly mobile, let alone chivalrous, armed forces. Anything not serving the war effort would have to be ruthlessly discarded, and this specifically included playing at politics. Politics would, in effect, be swallowed up by the war; the two would become indistinguishable. 'All the theories of Clausewitz should be thrown overboard … Both war and policy serve the existence of the nation. However, war is the highest expression of the people's will to live. Therefore politics must be made subordinate to war.' Or, to the extent that it was not, it was superfluous and, indeed, treasonable.

After 1945 Ludendorff's military thought was often attacked by featherweight commentators. In addition to taking a justified dislike to his racism and his early support for Hitler, they mistook *their* world – in which nuclear weapons had made total warfare as he understood it impossible – for his. During these years it was Liddell Hart and Fuller who, rightly or not, were celebrated as the fathers of the *Blitzkrieg* (whether Liddell Hart in particular had as much influence on its development as he later claimed has recently become the subject of an entire literature). Nevertheless, the fact remains that it was not their vision of the Second World War but Ludendorff's which turned out to be only too horribly true.

OPPOSITE: Ludendorff, 'who, like Atlas, had the strength to hold a world on his shoulders' (General von Blomberg, 1935), as he appeared in 1918 at the peak of his power.

Friedrich von Bernhardi was a Prussian general who at one time served as head of the Historical Department of the General Staff. In 1912 his book, How Germany Makes War, *established him as the country's leading militarist.*

In fulfilment of Douhet's vision, cities were bombed to the point that they were deserted even by birds, yet easy victory did not follow. These photographs show Nuremberg after its devastation in the Second World War and (below) after the war following its reconstruction.

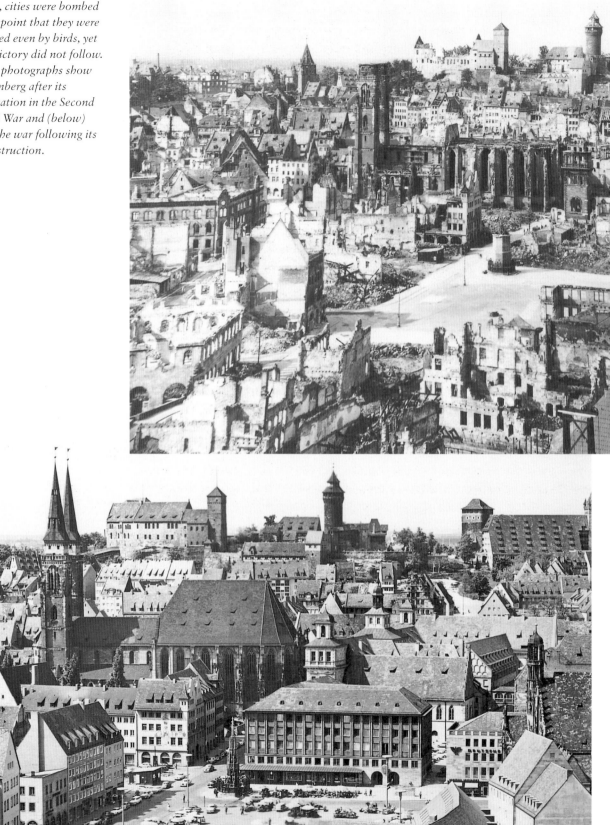

The war led to a vast expansion of bureaucracy: King George VI on a visit to the newly established Ministry of Food, 1940.

To be sure, fleets of aircraft did overfly fronts and bombed cities on a scale which, had he only been able to envisage it, might have made even Ludendorff blanch. Other aircraft, co-operating more closely with the tanks, helped carry out spectacular mobile operations on the ground. The combination of armour, mobility and wireless restored operational mobility, laying the groundwork for some spectacular victories in which countries the size of Poland and France were knocked down at a single blow. It also did much to re-establish the balance between defence and offence, although events were to show that both tanks and aircraft (the latter, thanks to the introduction of radar) were as capable of operating on the defence, and preventing a breakthrough, as they were of helping it to take place.

Where Ludendorff proved most correct, however, was in insisting that the Second World War – a term, of course, which he did not use – would be broadly like the first. As with its predecessor, it would develop into a gigantic struggle and a prolonged one. It would both demand and make possible the mobilization of all resources under a regime which, even in democratic countries, came pretty close to doing away with politics while putting everybody and everything under its own control (in 1945 the British Ministry of Food alone had no fewer than 30,000 employees). Ludendorff's posthumous triumph may, indeed, be seen in the fact that, by the time the war was over, a continent had been devastated and between forty and sixty million people lay dead. As the coming decades were to prove, the history of (conventional) military theory had run its course.

CHAPTER EIGHT

---•⋅∹⋅•◦◦▷◉◁◦◦•⋅∹⋅•---

FROM 1945 TO THE PRESENT

TO COMBAT GUERRILLA WARFARE US Air Force planes sprayed the Cambodian countryside with a herbicide, probably Agent Orange, to defoliate the area and expose Vietcong troops and fortifications, September 1966.

FROM 1945 TO THE PRESENT

THE FACT THAT THE Second World War had effectively put an end to conventional military theory was not evident at first. During the decades that followed a great many attempts were made to continue the debate, sometimes by men (there appear to be few if any women in the field) who had already made their mark before 1939. An enormous number of publications was produced and, almost as rapidly, forgotten. Of their authors none attained the prominence of a Fuller, let alone a Liddell Hart.

The paucity of first-rate theory is not difficult to explain. When the Gulf War broke out in 1991, forty-six years after Hiroshima, by far the most important motive power was still the internal combustion engine including, of course, jets. By far the most important formations were still those old and trusted World War products, i.e. squadrons of fighter bombers, armoured divisions, and, at sea, task-forces centring around aircraft-carriers and intended to achieve command of the sea (although, as it turned out, there was nobody to dispute it with). As both fighter bombers and armoured divisions operated by dropping or firing massive quantities of steel into the air, they were heavily dependent on lines of

The destruction of Hiroshima represented global war at its most ferocious, and at the same time put an end to such war.

communications for that steel as well as fuel; with the result that the objective of strategy remained, as it had been from the days of Buelow and Jomini, to cut those lines. To be sure, the forces were festooned with a great many other weapons and, as fashionable modern parlance has it, weapons systems. Missiles and cruise missiles and remotely piloted vehicles and helicopters, computers and data-links and satellites and global positioning systems: all these and more were employed. When everything was said and done, however, none proved capable of making the campaign very different from what, say, the German invasion of Poland in 1939 had been.

Between 1945 and 1991, faced with what was usually understood as unprecedented technological progress, many, perhaps the majority, of writers focused their efforts on the ways in which new weapons would be integrated into future war and influence its shape. Thus, in the 1950s and 1960s, it was often a question of coming to terms with the short- and medium-range missiles then coming into service (intercontinental missiles with their nuclear warheads are a different story and will be dealt with below). Later the 1973 Arab–Israeli war, which at the time was the most modern of its kind, led to a lively debate concerning the relative merits of armour and anti-tank missiles, air power and anti-aircraft defences, attack and defence, and quality versus quantity. Spurred on

After 1945, large-scale conventional war could only be fought between, or against, third-rate military powers: Israeli troops on the Golan Heights, October 1973.

by America's failure in Vietnam, which was blamed on the strategy of attrition adopted by the US armed forces, the 1980s saw a revival of conventional warfare theory centring around such ideas as 'manoeuvre warfare' and 'air–land battle'. As these terms imply, both focused on strategy and the operational art while all but ignoring grand strategy. Manoeuvre warfare took the German campaigns of the Second World War as its model, so much so that for some ten years 'German' and 'excellent' were considered synonymous, and ex-Wehrmacht generals were treated to free lunches at the Pentagon. Air–land battle could barely be distinguished from, say, what Patton and his supporting VIIth Tactical Air Force had done to the Wehrmacht at Falaise in 1944.

Throughout this period very great attention was naturally devoted to Soviet military theory and doctrine. As both they and their opponents in the Cold War never tired of pointing out, from Karl Marx the Soviets had inherited the idea that war was not just a military struggle. Instead it was a socio-economic phenomenon to be considered 'in its entirety', though just what this meant when it came to working out the details was not always clear. During the 1920s and 1930s Soviet authors such as Tukhachevsky seem to have drawn on their own experience in the Civil War and Soviet–Polish war, both of which had witnessed plenty of operational movement carried out by cavalry corps. With Fuller acting as the stimulant, mobility was married to mechanization. The outcome was something known as 'the battle in depth': meaning a highly offensive campaign

A detachment of the legendary Russian First Red Cavalry on the move, 1919.

which would be launched not merely along the front but against the enemy's communications, depots and command centres as well. Moreover, as Marxists the Soviets professed to have as much faith in 'the people' as Fuller and Douhet had been sceptical of them. If only for that reason, unlike their Western counterparts they never surrendered to the siren-song of small, élite armed forces.

Shortly after the battle of Moscow in 1941–2, i.e. at a time in which the Soviet Union had just gathered itself up from its initial defeats and begun to wage total war like no other country in history, Stalin promulgated the 'five permanently operating factors'. Not surprisingly they bore a strong family resemblance to the picture painted by Ludendorff six years previously – even to the point where one commentator claimed that the German general's doctrine was also capable of being summed up in five points. The most important factor was the political stability of the homeland, a phrase which, coming from under *that* particular moustache, might well make one shudder. This was followed by the morale of the armed forces, the quality and quantity of their divisions, armament, and the commanders' capacity for organizing the resources at their disposal. From then until the end of the Cold War, it was claimed that the best way to annihilate the enemy was by means of massive armoured offensives – much like, say, the ones which the Red Army had mounted against the Germans in 1943–5, only deeper, more powerful and better.

Over the decades, these debates provided a living for thousands if not tens of

The battle of Moscow formed the turning point of the Second World War. Soon after it was over, Stalin promulgated his doctrine of 'the five permanently operating principles'.

thousands of analysts, in and out of uniform. More important, on both sides of the Iron Curtain they fed vast military–industrial complexes which gave employment to millions and were not without influence both on the economies and on the political systems of the countries which they were supposed to serve. Overshadowing them all, however, was the question of nuclear weapons. The first atomic bomb dropped on Hiroshima was some fifteen hundred times as powerful as the largest weapon in existence until then. With the advent of hydrogen bombs the gap widened still further; but even when much smaller tactical nuclear weapons appeared on the scene the discrepancy between the two kinds of arms remained immense. In any attempt to understand the nature of future war and the way in which it should be conducted, the altogether unprecedented challenges posed by nuclear weapons have to be addressed first. Failure to do so was like discussing the activities of toddlers throwing pebbles at each other while the adults, machine-guns at the ready, stood by and watched.

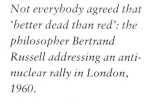

Not everybody agreed that 'better dead than red': the philosopher Bertrand Russell addressing an anti-nuclear rally in London, 1960.

In the event, the true significance of nuclear weapons was not understood at first. In part this was because there were not too many of them around; nor was it certain that the relatively few and slow bombers capable of carrying them would necessarily reach their targets. Hence it was excusable that many – although not all – senior politicians and military men in the West believed that the next war would be much like the last one, give or take a number of cities turned into radioactive wastes. In 1947, Stalin's previously mentioned picture of total war was reissued specifically with this message in mind. In the face of the American nuclear monopoly of the time, it had to be shown that 'adventurist' ideas could not succeed since other factors were even more decisive.

Previously in history, whenever some new and powerful weapon appeared on the scene, it had only been a question of time before it became fully incorporated into military doctrine and, as had happened in the case of the tank and the aircraft-carrier, was turned into the mainstay of that doctrine. From the late 1940s strenuous attempts were made to treat nuclear arms in the same

manner, i.e. devise ways for using them in war. First it was the US Air Force which, with its own interests as the sole organization capable of delivering the bomb to target very much in mind, demanded that nuclear bombardment be made the mainstay of American and Western defence, coming up with such aptly named operations as 'Bushwhacker', 'Dropshot' and 'Broiler'. Later the idea of 'Massive Retaliation' was adopted by the incoming Eisenhower administration. As Secretary of State John Foster Dulles declared in a famous speech, the US would not permit the other side to dictate the site and mode of the next war.

Instead, any attempt by the Communists to engage in aggression anywhere in the world *might* be instantly met with means, and at a place, of America's choosing.

By the time it was made, the credibility of this threat was already in some doubt. In September 1949 the Soviet Union had exploded its first atomic bomb and by the early 1950s its arsenal, though still smaller than that of the US, was growing. Given that the US was the first to develop operational H-bombs, possessed far more delivery vehicles and had *deployed* these delivery vehicles across a worldwide chain of bases, it could probably have 'won' a nuclear exchange; still this did not address the question as to what would happen if, in the face of an all-out offensive launched by the US air force and navy (which was also acquiring nuclear-capable aircraft), a few Soviet bombs somehow survived in their hideouts and, loaded aboard equally few bombers, found their way to North American targets such as New York and Washington DC. Then, as now, the Dr Strangeloves of this world tried to exorcize the 'bugaboo of radiation' and reassure the public that recovery from a nuclear war was possible. And then, as now, the question proved unanswerable.

In the late 1950s the situation changed again. Soviet nuclear power was growing, and so were the range and effectiveness of its delivery vehicles in the form of the first intercontinental ballistic missiles. The debate surrounding massive retaliation was replaced, or supplemented, by the question as to how the US itself could be protected against nuclear attack, leading to the emergence of terms such as 'city busting' and 'counter force', 'first strike' and 'second strike'. A broad consensus was formed that precisely because cities could not be protected against a nuclear offensive it was vital to have forces in place which could survive such an attack and still retaliate with sufficient force to wipe the other side off the map. The outcome was the famous Triad, a vast array of air-borne, sea-borne and land-based nuclear-strike forces linked together by an electronic command system and supposedly capable of 'riding out' anything that the Soviet Union could throw at them. Perhaps because the 1962 Missile Crisis had given people a fright, over time the Triad's role in fighting a war tended to be de-emphasized and its deterrent function was given greater prominence. Projected on to the other side, which in spite of its occasional protests to the contrary was supposed to share the same objective, this doctrine became known as 'Mutually Assured Destruction' or MAD.

A point to be made about these and other Western theories of nuclear power and its use in war is that, unlike the vast majority of their predecessors, they were produced neither by serving commanders nor by retired ones. To be sure, it was the generals who were left in charge of the armed forces themselves; building them, organizing and training them for action. From time to time one uniformed figure or another would also put his voice into the debate by penning an article or, more rarely, a book. Still, it was not they but civilian analysts – working either in the universities or, increasingly, in so-called think-tanks especially created for the purpose – who produced the most important 'strategic' volumes of the Cold

During the 1950s, the public was offered 'do-it-yourself' nuclear shelters, like this one.

War era: such as, to name but a few, Albert Wholstetter's *Selection and Use of Strategic Air Bases* (1954, with F. S. Hoffman, R. J. Lutz, and H. S. Rowen), William Kaufman's *Military Policy and National Security* (1956), Henry Kissinger's *Nuclear Weapons and Foreign Policy* (1957), Robert Osgood's *Limited War*, Herman Kahn's *On Thermonuclear War* (1960) and Thomas Schelling's *Arms and Influence* (1966). Though ostensibly dealing with 'strategy', all these works were concerned at least as much with deterring war as with devising better ways to fight it. As the title suggests, the last in particular all but renounced the use of armed force as suicidal; instead it explained how a state might avail itself of a nuclear arsenal to exercise diplomatic pressure on its opponent while itself resisting similar pressure. It was as if war itself had been cut down to size. To misuse a phrase coined by an earlier head of state, in the face of weapons literally capable of destroying the earth, war had become too dangerous to leave to the generals.

From time to time, the question was raised as to whether the balance of terror might not be upset, and a capability for at least limited war-fighting restored, by devising some kind of defensive umbrella. As early as October 1945 a Canadian general went on record as saying that the means for countering the atomic bomb were 'clearly in sight' – a premature statement, no doubt, but one which has since then been repeated countless times. In the late 1950s communities and people were encouraged to provide themselves with anti-nuclear shelters, and advertisements for such shelters, looking just like the typical American living room magically transported underground, were circulated. The late 1960s

SOVIET AND AMERICAN BLOCS 1957–67

Between 1945 and 1991 the two superpowers confronted each other, deploying an awesome array of nuclear weapons capable of being launched from the land, the air, and the sea. As the range of the delivery vehicles grew, ultimately no place in either the US or the USSR remained safe from them.

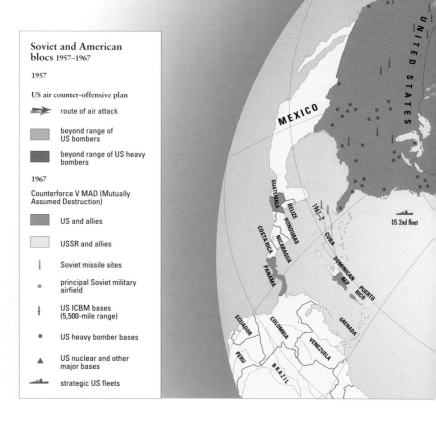

Soviet and American blocs 1957–1967

1957

US air counter-offensive plan

➤ route of air attack

■ beyond range of US bombers

■ beyond range of US heavy bombers

1967

Counterforce V MAD (Mutually Assumed Destruction)

■ US and allies

■ USSR and allies

| Soviet missile sites

■ principal Soviet military airfield

| US ICBM bases (5,500-mile range)

■ US heavy bomber bases

▲ US nuclear and other major bases

strategic US fleets

brought ABM, or anti-ballistic missiles, the idea being to 'hit a bullet with a bullet' – as the phrase went – and intercept the incoming Soviet missiles while still *en route*. The advent of MIRV (multiple independent re-entry vehicles), of which more below, terminated those hopes. In 1972 it led to the Strategic Arms Limitation Treaty (SALT), which obliged both sides to agreed not to deploy anti-ballistic missiles; however, in 1983, President Reagan's so-called Star Wars initiative once again aimed at rendering ballistic missiles 'impotent and obsolete'. Each time billions of dollars were sunk into the effort. Each time, too, it turned

THE BOEING B-52 STRATOFORTRESS

First operational in the early 1960s, the Boeing B-52, with its 12,000-kilometre (7,500-mile) range, was capable of delivering nuclear weapons to almost any part of the Soviet Union.

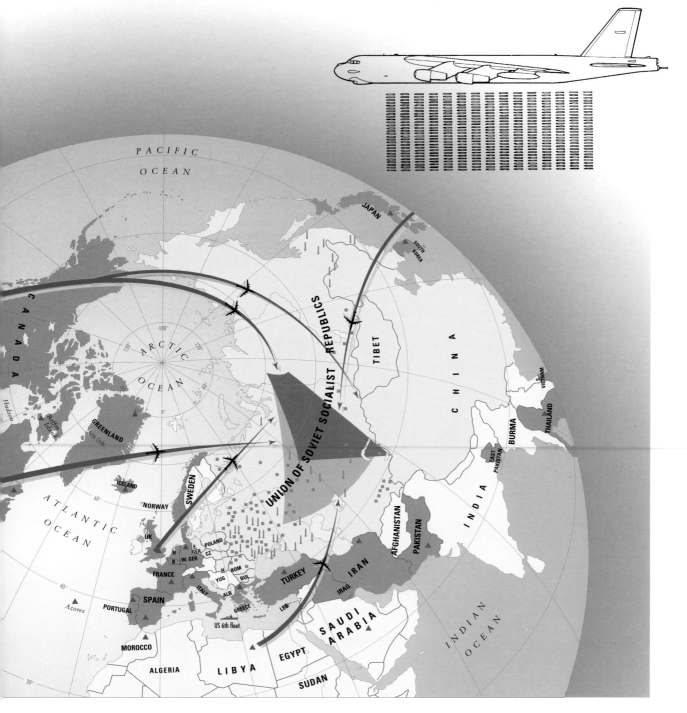

'In the face of weapons literally capable of destroying the earth, war had become too dangerous to leave to the generals': an underwater atomic test, 1957.

A nuclear delivery vehicle that gained prominence during the 1970s was the cruise missile. So far, though, they have only been used to carry conventional warheads.

So far, all attempts to render nuclear weapons 'impotent and obsolete' (President Reagan, referring to the Strategic Defense Initiative) have failed. Instead, the balance of terror led to arms reduction agreements, such as the one here being signed by Reagan and Gorbachev in 1987.

out that anything even resembling 'reliable' protection was out of reach. Not, perhaps, because it could not be done from a technical point of view, but because, set in the context of nuclear weapons which are quite capable of annihilating entire societies in a second, 'protection' and 'reliable' constituted an oxymoron.

Running in parallel with the attempts to design a defence was the progressive introduction of smaller 'tactical' nuclear weapons. Capable of being carried by a variety of delivery vehicles – from fighter-bombers down to atomic bazookas – they raised the question whether they might not be used against at least some targets without running the risk of blowing up the world; whether, in other words, nuclear warfare, once it had broken out, could not be contained within a single theatre. Towards the late 1960s the same question was raised with even greater urgency by the near-simultaneous appearance of two new technologies, MIRV and cruise missiles. Besides putting an end to any hope that incoming missiles might be intercepted – given that each missile was now made to carry as many as ten warheads – both MIRV and cruise missiles were capable of delivering those warheads with unprecedented accuracy, 'straight through Mr Brezhnev's window'. Both therefore gave rise to hopes, if that is the word, that a nuclear war might be fought without necessarily leading to escalation. On paper at any rate, the outcome was a shift away from deterrence towards possible use of nuclear weapons in war; from the early 1970s to the mid-1980s there was much talk of 'flexible response', 'selected options', 'escalation dominance', 'decapitation', and even something known as 'nuclear shots across the bow'.

Since the Korean war the rationale behind the various American attempts to find ways for using nuclear weapons in war was the considerable gap in conventional forces believed to exist between the US and the USSR. From at least the time of the publication of V. D. Sokolovsky's *Soviet Military Strategy* (1961), the standard Soviet response was that the Americans were deluding themselves. Any war between the superpowers would be full-scale from the beginning; it would involve the use of all available nuclear

In 1961, General Sokolovsky provided the most comprehensive statement ever of Soviet nuclear doctrine.

weapons not only at the front but, as Soviet doctrine dictated and Soviet organization implied, in depth as well. Whether, had war broken out, the Soviet threat to escalate would have proved more credible than the American attempt to make first use of nuclear weapons possible by limiting its scope is questionable; but it certainly served the objective – if that, in fact, was its objective – to deter war. One way or another, and in spite of countless crises, forty years of Cold War during which both superpowers behaved like scorpions in a bottle did not end in a nuclear exchange; by some interpretations, such an exchange had never even been close. No matter how often it was announced that new and much more accurate weapons had brought about the death of MAD, in practice it proved remarkably hard to escape. As Bernhard Brodie wrote in *The Absolute Weapon* as far back as 1946: 'Thus far the chief purpose of a military establishment has been to win wars. From now on, its chief purpose must be to avert them. It can have no other useful purpose.'

Guerrilla warfare could be waged even in the teeth of the most powerful military technology ever: a scene from the Vietnam War, 1963.

Before 1914 Lawrence of Arabia had been a student of archaeology at Oxford. During the war he became a guerrilla leader. His book about the experience, The Seven Pillars of Wisdom, *became a best-seller. Here he is shown on a camel, with a companion.*

As additional countries joined the nuclear club – by 1998 there were at least eight, plus any number which were capable of building the bomb had they felt the need to do so – the logic of deterrence began to work for them too. Contrary to the fears expressed by many Western strategists, this turned out to be true regardless of whether they were democratic West Europeans, or Communist Chinese, or Indians claiming to have inherited Mahatma Gandhi's doctrine of *ahimsa* (non-violence), or Pakistanis seeking an 'Islamic bomb', or Jews allegedly possessed by a 'Holocaust complex'; regardless also whether the nuclear arsenals in question were small or large, primitive or sophisticated, balanced by those of the enemy or not. For a country to wage large-scale war against a nuclear enemy without the aid of nuclear weapons was madness; to do so with nuclear weapons, greater madness still. From the late 1960s, any country in possession of the industrial and technological resources necessary for waging large-scale conventional war was also able to build nuclear weapons. Hence, and not surprisingly, there was a growing tendency for such war to be fought solely by, or against, third- and fourth-rate military powers – the latest case in point being, as of the time of writing, Ethiopia and Eritrea.

This is not to say that nuclear weapons were capable of deterring *all* sorts of war. In particular, the post-1945 era has witnessed a great many wars which were fought not by states against each other but inside them, at the hand of non-state actors variously known as militias, guerrillas or terrorists. Waged not by regular forces invading across some border but at extremely close quarters by people who could barely be distinguished from the surrounding civilian populations, these wars were impervious to nuclear threats. Moreover, as experience in Vietnam, Afghanistan and countless other places was to show, they could be waged even in the teeth of the most powerful conventional forces in history. Considering that entire continents, and hundreds of millions if not billions of people, came to live under different political regimes as a direct result of such wars, there could be no doubt about their effectiveness; no wonder that they multiplied promiscuously.

Guerrilla warfare, of course, is nothing new. Throughout history, people too weak to meet their opponents in open battle have resorted to attacking them by stealth, sometimes winning the struggle but more often losing it as ruthless countermeasures, including turning entire districts into deserts, were taken. Nevertheless, the first attempts to formulate a guerrilla *theory* had to wait until the second half of the eighteenth century. And even then the term referred not to a 'people's war' as we understand it but to what was also known as *Kleinkrieg* or *petite guerre*, meaning the operations of small groups of troops who engaged on the sidelines, so to speak, and were beneath the notice of that novel, mysterious and august doctrine, strategy.

A coherent theory of guerrilla warfare was, perhaps, put together for the first time by Lawrence of Arabia in *The Seven Pillars of Wisdom* (1926). A typical eccentric – when used to describe the products of Britain's public school system the two terms are not as contradictory as might be thought at first sight – before 1914 he had studied archaeology at Oxford. During the war he found himself working for British Intelligence in Cairo and it was in this capacity that he was first sent to what is today Saudi Arabia in order to foment a revolt against Ottoman rule. In his book he sought to recapitulate his experiences as one of the leaders of that revolt in 1916–18, though whether his contribution to it was really as great as he and his adoring followers tried to make out has subsequently been questioned.

To Lawrence, then, the guerrillas ought to operate 'like a cloud of gas'. Most of the time they should be inactive and invisible, hiding in places too remote and inaccessible to be reached by their larger and more cumbersome opponents and relying on dispersion and mobility in order to escape such punitive expeditions as might be sent against them. Such expeditions, however, might also provide opportunities for action, given that regular forces would inevitably rely on lines of communication which could be subjected to attack. In general, guerrillas ought to avoid head-on clashes with the enemy's main body. Instead they were to operate against his flanks, his foraging parties, the garrisons which he put into isolated places and the like, all the while relying on speed and surprise to concentrate their own forces, do their worst and disappear again before reinforcements could be brought up and retaliatory action taken. Logistically speaking they were to be sustained partly from the countryside and partly by taking arms and equipment away from the enemy, thus making it unnecessary to have permanent, and vulnerable, bases. So far, the theory; however, it should by no means be overlooked that throughout the revolt Lawrence and his ally, Shariff Hussein of Mecca, received both money and weapons from British Military Headquarters in Egypt.

As will be evident from the above account, Lawrence was concerned above all with the tactical and operational – assuming the latter term is applicable at all – aspects of guerrilla warfare. In this respect, subsequent authors have added little to his work; after all, there are only so many ways of saying that 'when the enemy advances, we retreat'. What the other important writer on guerrilla warfare, Mao Tse-tung, did add was, first, an analysis of the relationship between the guerrillas and the people at large and, second, his famous 'three-stage' theory of the way in which the campaign ought to proceed. Dependent as the guerrillas were on the people for shelter and supply, the indispensable condition for obtaining success consisted of gaining the support of that people. This might be done by propaganda, by deliberately provoking the enemy into reprisals or by main force ('power grows from the barrel of a gun'); in the case of main force, good care

The Afghan guerrillas here shown may not have belonged to any regular army, but they did defeat the strongest military power ever to bestride the planet. Ultimately, the defeat in Afghanistan even contributed to the disintegration of the USSR.

should be taken not to allow the guerrillas to become simply a group of marauders. Whatever the method or methods used, the essential point to grasp is that the struggle is primarily *political* by nature.

Drawing on his own experiences as leader of China's civil war, Mao, followed by his Vietnamese student Giap, believed that the first phase ought to consist of isolated hit-and-run attacks against enemy forces, with the aim of weakening and demoralizing them. The second phase would witness the consolidation of guerrilla power in some remote, outlying and difficult area to access; from there they would continue their work of propaganda, harassment and sabotage. Once the enemy had been sufficiently weakened and started to retreat, the guerrillas, embarking on the third phase of their campaign, would resort to open warfare. The real trick was to select carefully the moment for this phase to begin. If launched too early it might lead to disaster as a still powerful enemy hit back; if delayed for too long, the seeming endlessness of the struggle might cause the guerrillas themselves to become demoralized.

To Lawrence, then, guerrilla warfare was mainly another form of military action. To Mao, by contrast, it was above all a question of drawing 'the masses' to one's own side and mobilizing them. Given that there are clear limits to both indoctrination and force, this in turn meant the implementation of economic and social reforms amounting to revolution or, to call it by another frequently used name, people's war. War and politics thus became inseparable; though in practice Communist-led guerrilla movements in particular always took very good care to ensure that the will of the Party, and not that of the military cadres, should prevail. Meanwhile the fact that social, economic and military means were not so much used as a tool of politics as fused with it made it very hard to fit guerrilla warfare and its smaller offshoot, terrorism, into the accepted Clausewitzian framework – as Mao (to judge by his remark referred to on page 123) may have realized. Nor did guerrilla warfare offer nearly as much scope for powerful concentrations of troops and decisive battles against the enemy's main forces as the Prussian writer would have liked to have seen. As a result, since 1945 general works which tried to get to grips with the nature of war have very often devoted a separate chapter to guerrilla warfare as if it stood in no relation to anything else.

Ludendorff excepted, since the 1830s the most important theoretical framework by far had been the one presented by Clausewitz. Moltke, Schlieffen, von Bernhardi, von der Goltz and Foch, Fuller and Liddell Hart (in so far as he accepted that the purpose of war was to serve the political objectives of the state), and the Marxists and many of the advocates of limited nuclear war: all these could trace their intellectual origins to the great Prussian and, in many cases, were all the more prepared to acknowledge their debt the less they read him and understood his views. However, by 1990 at the latest, the Clausewitzian framework was beginning to show serious cracks. As has just been said, it proved incapable of incorporating warfare by, or against, non-state actors, and indeed Clausewitz himself, in the five pages which he devotes to the subject, had treated

AP BAC, VIETNAM

The battle of Ap Bac, December 1963, set the pattern for the Vietnam War. A South Vietnamese Army formation hit upon the Vietcong but, instead of *fighting it out, acted in the most incompetent manner possible and allowed the enemy to escape. The battle set the stage for the infusion of many more US troops into* *Vietnam. It was typical of most of its successors in that the Vietcong guerrillas always proved much more nimble than their heavily armed opponents.*

1. Original Vietcong positions

2. 1st Battalion of civil guard arrives. Concealed Vietcong open fire. Civil guard falls back in disorder, their commanding officer among the killed

3. US advisor flying overhead in spotter plane orders helicopter-borne infantry reinforcements

4. These reinforcements land too close to the Vietcong positions. Many are wounded and survivors withdraw

5. Sky raider fighter-bombers launch napalm attack but hit villages and miss Vietcong positions

6. In an attempt to rescue the downed helicopter crews, armoured personnel carriers are ordered forward. Thought invulnerable to small arms fire, the carriers approach the eastern tree line. At point-blank range the Vietcong open fire, killing machine gunners riding on the vehicles. The Vietcong then rush forward throwing grenades and the carriers withdraw

7. The senior American advisor still flying overhead persuades the South Vietnamese commander to order a parachute drop to seal in the Vietcong. The drop is badly handled and the troops land in front of the Vietcong positions and come under heavy fire. They are therefore unable to launch an attack

8. 7th South Vietnamese infantry division approaching from the north are unable to co-operate with dispersed and pinned down airborne troops

9. During the night the Vietcong withdraw, having tied down a force many times their size and vastly better equipped. In the process only eighteen of their own men were killed

guerrilla warfare solely as an extension of the struggle between states. At the same time, the question could not be avoided whether his insistence on the inherent tendency of war to escalate made him into a fit guide to nuclear-armed military establishments, one of whose objectives, if not the most important one, had always been deterrence rather than war-fighting. So long as the Cold War lasted, and with it at least the possibility of large-scale conventional hostilities between the superpowers, these doubts were suppressed. Interpreted as the prophet of limited war, all too often Clausewitz was presented almost as if he were a tweed-clad, slipper-wearing, pipe-smoking Western analyst. It was no accident that none was more enthusiastic about him than precisely the so-called 'military reformers' who, throughout the 1980s, sought to bring about a revival of 'manoeuvre war' theory.

During the Vietnam War the US employed all the most modern weapons available at the time. The 6 million tons of bombs dropped proved no more effective in halting the Vietcong than the bombing of Kosovo could prevent ethnic cleansing there thirty years later.

As the millennium comes to an end, two opposing visions of future war seem to be receiving widespread support. One of these still sticks to the framework first created by Clausewitz. Along with the master, it starts from the assumption that war will continue to be used mainly as an instrument of policy at the hand of one state against another. Since reliable defences against nuclear weapons are still not on the horizon, tacitly or explicitly this school finds itself compelled to pretend that they do *not* exist. Thus, at one 1997 conference which dealt with the so-called RMA (revolution in military affairs), a videotape of an imaginary future news broadcast was shown. Cast against the background of Tower Bridge, London, the announcer pretended to be speaking in the year AD 2020; he started by saying that nuclear weapons had just been abolished.

The danger of nuclear annihilation having been swept away by the stroke of the pen, American analysts in particular talk happily about physical warfare being supplemented by, or even abolished in favour of, 'information warfare'. Just as the introduction of aircraft during the early years of the twentieth century added a third dimension to warfare, it is argued, so future hostilities will extend into a fourth dimension known as 'cyberspace'. The electronic circuitry needed for waging information war will be taken straight off the shelves of any electronics store, a proposition which, incidentally, ignores the fact that a single nuclear weapon by virtue of generating an electro-magnetic pulse (EMP) is quite

capable of wiping out the communications and data-processing systems of an
entire country. The actual conduct of the war will be entrusted to uniformed
hackers. Sitting behind screens and hitting buttons, instead of targeting the
enemy's men and weapons in the field, they will seek to spoof or jam or saturate
the enemy's sensors, disrupt his communications and infiltrate his computers,
thus rendering him blind, deaf and mute.

The other school, to which the present author belongs, argues that the
proliferation of nuclear weapons has all but brought large-scale interstate warfare
to an end. (If nuclear weapons are not used, then large-scale conventional
interstate warfare appears to be finished; if they *are* used, then it will already be
finished.) Therefore, although isolated attempts to break into the C^3 (or C-cube:
command, control, communications) systems of military establishments around
the world cannot be excluded and in fact have already been made, large-scale

The Grand Hotel in Brighton, southern England, after a terrorist bombing.

information warfare waged by one state against an equally sophisticated opponent relying on computers, electronic communications and sensors is increasingly unlikely. Designed, financed and maintained by one state for the purpose of fighting another, present-day armed forces are dinosaurs about to disappear; in quantitative terms, and compared with their size at any point since 1945, most of them have already all but disappeared. Furthermore, whereas Clausewitz and his followers looked at war as an instrument in the hands of policy, in fact it is not primarily a rational instrument for the achievement of rational goals. At a deeper level, it would be more correct to say that those goals themselves are but excuses for man's natural desire to fight.

Britain lost more people to the IRA than during the Suez campaign, the Falklands War and the Gulf War put together, leading to the proliferation of posters such as this one.

SMART BOMBING

By the time the Kosovo air campaign was launched in 1999, only a single country still possessed bombers. Their place had been taken by smaller, more agile, fighter-bombers such as the F-16 here shown, which were armed with precision guided weapons.

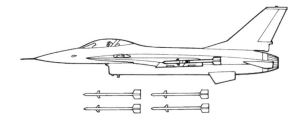

War by television

⚓	naval forces
✈	sea launch missiles
✈	airstrikes from bases in Italy
💥	major targets

WAR BY TELEVISION

A map of Serbia showing the main characteristics of the NATO air campaign in the spring of 1999.

Hence the fact that nuclear weapons are inexorably pushing large-scale inter-state warfare under the carpet, so to speak, should in no way be mistaken for the end of war as such; as Fuller wrote in a footnote to the preface of *Armaments and History* (1946), 'one does not eradicate the causes of war by obliterating cities'. As Afghanistan and Algeria, Bosnia and Rwanda, and countless other places prove, *Warre* in its elemental Hobbesian sense is not only alive and well but as deadly as ever. Nor should one succumb to the fashionable assumption – which itself is not without its historical predecessors from Edward Gibbon to Norman Angel – that such struggles are necessarily confined to less civilized (read 'developing') countries: Britain for example lost more people to the IRA than during the Suez campaign, the Falklands War and the Gulf War put together. Breaking out now here, now there, limited in geographical scope but often extremely bloody, future war will be waged overwhelmingly by, and against, organizations that are not states. And since they do not own sovereign territory and consequently cannot be threatened with nuclear annihilation, they will be able to fight each other, and the state, to their heart's content.

'As Plato wrote long ago, the only people who will no longer see war are the dead': Latin translation of the dialogues dedicated to Lorenzo de Medici, Italy, c. 1480.

At the time of writing, which of the two visions will prove correct remains to be seen. Each one, but particularly the first, which enjoys the institutionalized support of the armed forces of the sole superpower left on earth, has already been made into the subject of a vast body of literature. However large the literature, it is perhaps true to say that, with the exception of the present author's *Transformation of War* (1991), so far neither school has attempted to present a comprehensive theory that will go back to first principles while at the same time offering a practical guide to the future. And yet, as the countless failures of the world's state-owned, regular armed forces to put down guerrillas and insurgents show, such a theory is urgently needed. 'The end of history' is not in sight, and indeed Francis Fukuyama (the author of that thesis) would be the first to agree that eternal peace might not satisfy those specimens of the human race who are affected by what he calls *megalotimia*, a hankering for great things. As Plato wrote long ago, the only people who will no longer see war are the dead.

SOME LEADING MILITARY THINKERS

AENEAS THE TACTICIAN (fourth century BC)
Wrote an extremely comprehensive, if somewhat pedestrian, guide to the conduct of war at the technical and tactical levels.

ASCLEPIODOTUS (first century BC)
Wrote an essay on tactics that may have originated as a philosophical exercise. It contains an extremely pedantic discussion of the structure of the Greek phalanx.

BERENHORST, GEORG HEINRICH (1733–1814)
Prussian author who reacted against the Enlightenment view of war as a rational activity, emphasizing the importance of moral factors.

BONET, HONORÉ (*c.* 1400)
The representative *par excellence* of the chivalric tradition whose *Tree of Battles* tries to lay down a comprehensive system as to what is, and is not, permissible in war.

BUELOW, ADAM HEINRICH VON (1752–1807)
German writer who was the first to describe strategy in terms of bases and lines of communication. Though he went too far in his use of geometry, he was one of the most original military thinkers ever.

CLAUSEWITZ, CARL VON (1780–1831)
Prussian General who combined Buelow's thoughts on strategy with Berenhorst's emphasis on war as a question of chracter above all. The result, *On War*, is probably the most famous ever on the subject.

CORBETT, JULIAN (1854–1922)
English writer on naval affairs. His *Some Principles of Naval Strategy* emphasized the political uses of sea power and served as a useful corrective to Mahan's famous *Influence*.

DOUHET, GIULIO (1869–1930)
Italian general and writer on air strategy. His 1921 book on that subject, *The Command of the Air*, is certainly the most famous one ever written. Some would argue that its vision was fully realized for the first time during the 1991 Gulf War.

DU PICQ, ARDANT (1819–70)
French officer who studied the behaviour of men in battle. Published as *Combat Studies*, his work became the intellectual basis for late nineteenth-century French military doctrine.

ENGELS, FRIEDRICH (1820–95)
Marx's good friend and fellow-worker, Engels specialized in military history and theory. He published numerous articles which are taken as the basis of the Marxist doctrine of war.

FOLARD, JEAN CHARLES (1669–1752)
French soldier and writer on military affairs. Sought to show that, in the age of muskets and linear tactics, a phalanx based on the Macedonian one was still viable.

FREDERICK II, OF PRUSSIA (reigned 1740–86)
King of Prussia and one of the greatest commanders in history. Wrote several works on the art of war, with the emphasis on the relationship among the various arms.

FRONTINUS, SEXTUS JULIUS (late first century AD)
Roman administrator and soldier. His *Strategemata*, a collection of ruses used by various commanders at various times and places, was famous throughout the Middle Ages.

FULLER, JOHN FREDERICK (1878–1964)
British soldier. In the First World War he served as chief of staff to the Royal Tank Corps. In the 1920s and 1930s he popularized the idea that tanks would form the wave of the future.

GUIBERT, JACQUES ANTOINE (1743–90)
French writer on military affairs whose works in some ways foreshadowed the revolution in warfare brought about by Napoleon.

JOMINI, ANTOINE HENRI (1779–1869)
French soldier of Swiss origin. During the first half of the nineteenth century his writings were considered to be *the* guide to the conduct of war in general and to strategy in particular.

LEO, CALLED THE WISE, EMPEROR (reigned 890–912)
Supposed author of the *Tacticon*, a Byzantine military handbook. It is based on the *Strategikon* and also contains entire passages lifted straight out of Onasander.

LIDDELL HART, BASIL HENRY (1895–1970)
British pundit. Author of *Strategy* (originally published 1929), probably the most famous twentieth-century work on conventional warfare. Claimed to be, and was regarded by some as, the father of the German *Blitzkrieg* in the Second World War.

LUDENDORFF, ERICH (1865–1937)
German soldier who was in charge of his country's army during the First World War. After the war he founded a publishing house which, along with assorted anti-Semitic tracts, published his *The Nation at War*, in which he set forth his vision of future total war.

MACHIAVELLI, NICCOLÒ (1469–1527)
Italian Renaissance writer, (in)famous author of *The Prince*. His work *The Art of War* was famous in his time, but probably does not deserve to be included among the true classics.

MAHAN, ALFRED (1840–1914)
American naval officer and writer on naval affairs. His principal book, *The Influence of Seapower upon History*, is the most famous naval treatise ever.

MAURICE, EMPEROR (reigned 582–602)
Supposed author of the *Strategikon*, a comprehensive guide to military affairs. Very good on organization, logistics, training and equipment, as well as stratagems of every kind.

MOLTKE, HELMUT VON (1800–91)
German soldier. As chief of the General Staff, he masterminded the campaigns against Austria (1866) and France (1871). His theoretical writings on war consist of numerous memoranda in which he emphasized the importance of railways, telegraphs, firepower, external lines and the need to improvise; in his own words, 'strategy is a system of expedients'.

MONTECUCCOLI, RAIMONDO (1609–80)
Italian nobleman and soldier who served the Habsburgs during and after the Thirty Years War. Probably the first writer to treat war as the continuation of state policy.

ONASANDER (first century AD)
Onasander, who like Asclepiodotus seems to have been a student of philosophy, wrote a treatise on the qualities which a general should have and how he should exercise his office. On the whole it is sensible and well balanced, but intellectually unexciting and totally lacking in examples.

PISAN, CHRISTINE DE (1364–1430)
French medieval writer who, among other things, composed a work called the *Art of Chivalry*.

PUYSEGUR, FRANÇOIS DE CHASTENET (1655–1743)
French soldier; served as quartermaster to the army of Louis XIV. Wrote a book whose purpose was to put field warfare on the same scientific basis as siege warfare.

SAXE, MAURICE DE (1696–1750)
French commander-in-chief during the War of the Austrian Succession. In 1732 he wrote – allegedly within thirteen feverish nights – a book which soon became famous and which in many ways epitomizes eighteenth-century warfare.

SCHELLING, THOMAS (1918–)
American professor of political science, Harvard University. His 1966 work, *Arms and Influence*, is the best ever published on nuclear strategy.

SCHLIEFFEN, ALFRED VON (1833–1913)
Chief of the German General Staff from 1893 to 1905. His writings, all of which were meant to justify the plan he conceived for defeating France, emphasized the importance of outflanking movements.

SOKOLOVSKY, VASILY DANILOVICH (1897–1968)
Soviet field marshal who gained his spurs in the Second World War. In 1962 he headed a group of officers who published the most comprehensive statement of Soviet military doctrine ever.

SUN TZU (first half of fifth century BC)
Chinese commander and author of *The Art of War*. Based on the premise that war is an evil and emphasizing deceit, this is the best work on war ever.

VAUBAN, SÉBASTIEN LE PRESTRE DE (1633–1707)
French soldier. An expert on fortification and siegecraft, he wrote *The Attack and Defense of Places*, which, besides being a model of its kind, also served as a starting point for Enlightenment military thought in general.

VEGETIUS, RENATUS FLAVIUS (late fourth century AD)
Roman officer, author of an essay called *Things Military* that emphasizes organization and tactics. Alhough it does not present the Roman army as it was at any particular time, the book became a classic and remained in use throughout the Middle Ages and the Renaissance.

FURTHER READING

GENERAL

Up to now, there has been no attempt to cover the whole of military theory in a single volume; moreover, existing accounts tend to distinguish between Western, Chinese and Byzantine military theory as if they existed on different planets. What are available are several good volumes on Western military theory, beginning approximately with the Renaissance and ending almost at the present day. Still, even of those, only one has been written by a single author (the rest are collective works) and that one only covers the period from 1790.

Earle, E. M. (ed.), *Makers of Modern Strategy* (Princeton, NJ, 1943).

Howard, M. (ed.), *The Theory and Practice of War* (Bloomington, Ind., 1965).

Paret, P. (ed.), *Makers of Modern Strategy from Machiavelli to the Nuclear Age* (Princeton, NJ, 1986).

Semmel, B., *Marxism and the Science of War* (New York, 1981).

Wallach, J. L., *Kriegstheorien, ihre Entwicklung im 19. und 20. Jahrhundert* (Frankfurt am Main, 1972).

CHAPTER 1. CHINESE MILITARY THOUGHT

In recent years, the spread of low-intensity warfare and the consequent problems that face a Clausewitzian understanding of war have caused the Chinese classics to make a comeback. There are currently at least four different translations of Sun Tzu on the market; others have been translated for the first time. The growing interest in Chinese military theory has also led to some attempts to compare Sun Tzu with the greatest Western theorist, Karl von Clausewitz.

Grinter, L. E., 'Cultural and Historical Influences on Conflict in Sinic Asia: China, Japan, and Vietnam', in S. J. Blank and others (eds.), *Conflict and Culture in History* (Washington DC, 1993), pp. 117–92.

Handel, M., *Masters of War: Sun Tzu, Clausewitz, and Jomini* (London, 1992).

Sun Pin, *Military Methods* (Boulder, Colo., 1995).

The Seven Military Classics of Ancient China (Boulder, Colo., 1993).

CHAPTER 2. FROM ANTIQUITY TO THE MIDDLE AGES

As will be evident from the fact that almost all the sources for this chapter are primary, very few modern scholars have paid serious attention to ancient, Byzantine, or medieval military thought. I find it hard to think why this is the case; on the other hand, these are fields in which students who are out to make their name may well be able to do so.

Aeneas, *Tacticus* (London, 1948).

Asclepiodotus, *Tactics* (London, 1948).

Bonet, H., *The Tree of Battles* (Liverpool, 1949).

Contamine, Ph., *War in the Middle Ages* (Oxford, 1984).

Frontinus, Julius Sextus, *Strategemata* (London, 1950).
Maurice, Emperor, *Strategikon* (Philadelphia, Pa., 1984).
Onasander, *The General* (London, 1948).
Three Byzantine Military Treatises (Washington DC, 1985).
Vegetius, Renatus Flavius, *Epitoma Rei Militaris* (Liverpool, 1993).

CHAPTER 3. FROM 1500 TO 1763

From the time of the Renaissance, and following the introduction of print, the number of essays on military theory that saw the light of day grew by leaps and bounds. As to the secondary literature, it is extremely scattered, being contained in numerous articles and consequently reaching only the specialist; its quantity, however, is overwhelming. It is because of the *surfeit* of material, rather than its absence, that the items listed below are all primary.

Barker, T. M., *The Military Intellectual and Battle* (Albany, NY, 1975).
J. Luvaas (ed.), *Frederick the Great on the Art of War* (New York, 1966).
Machiavelli, N., *The Art of War*, in *Machiavelli, The Chief Works and Others*, vol. 2 (Durham, NC, 1965).
Puysegur, J. F. de Chastenet, *L'Art de la guerre par des principes et des règles* (Paris, 1748).
de Saxe, M., *Reveries or Memoirs upon the Art of War* (Westport, Conn., 1971).

CHAPTER 4. FROM GUIBERT TO CLAUSEWITZ

In the West, and for reasons that are still not entirely clear, the period between 1770 and 1830 saw military thought climb to heights never reached before or since. An entire new plane of war, known as strategy, was invented; particularly on the philosophical level (which was often entirely absent from previous works, the Chinese excepted), much of what was written at that time remains directly relevant to the present day. The following is but a small selection of the primary and secondary literature.

Buelow, A. H. D. von, *The Spirit of the Modern System of War* (London, 1806).
Clausewitz, K. von, *On War*, M. Howard and P. Paret (eds.) (Princeton, NJ, 1976).
Gat, A., *Clausewitz and the Enlightenment: the Origins of Modern Military Thought* (Oxford, 1988).
Handel, M. (ed.), *Clausewitz and Modern Strategy* (London, 1986).
Jomini, A. H., *Summary of the Art of War* (New York, 1854).
Paret, P., *Clausewitz and the State* (Princeton, NJ, 1976).

CHAPTER 5. THE NINETEENTH CENTURY

Compared with the period before 1830, the 'long' nineteenth century which ended in 1914 produced few first-class works on military theory. This was no accident: most writers considered themselves disciples first of Jomini and then, after 1870 or so, of Clausewitz. In one respect, however, nineteenth-century military theory was distinctly modern and entirely different from its predecessors. Against the background of the Industrial Revolution, it had to concern itself – and often did concern itself – not just with individual technological devices but with technological *change*. This concern in turn reflected a new understanding of history that was born around 1790 and, except for those of us who are 'postmodernist', is still the dominant one today.

Ardant du Picq, C. J. J., *Battle Studies: Ancient and Modern Battle* (New York, 1921).

Bernhardi, Th. von, *Germany and the Next War* (New York, 1914).

Bloch, I. H., *The Future of War* (Boston, Mass., 1903).

Foch, F., *De la conduite de la guerre* (Paris, 1903).

Goltz, C. von der, *The Nation in Arms* (London, 1913).

Gat, A., *The Development of Military Thought: the Nineteenth Century* (Oxford, 1992).

Hughes, D. M. (ed.), *Moltke on the Art of War* (Novato, Calif., 1993).

Schlieffen, A. von, *Cannae* (Berlin, 1936).

CHAPTER 6. NAVAL WARFARE

The study of naval warfare has rarely attracted any first-class minds; perhaps this was because, for most of history, it was seen primarily as an adjunct to operations on land. In any case it was only at the end of the nineteenth century that it found its first great theorist in the person of Captain Alfred T. Mahan. Mahan's vision was challenged by Julian Corbett, whose work puts more emphasis on the political uses of seapower. Since then, though there exist a huge number of specialized studies, nothing comparable has emerged; perhaps the most significant single contribution was Gorshkov's *The Seapower of the State*, but even that is merely a collection of articles and owed more to its author's position as chief of the Soviet navy than to any inherent intellectual qualities.

Corbett, J., *Some Principles of Maritime Strategy* (New York, 1972).

Gorshkov, S. G., *The Seapower of the State* (Oxford, 1979).

Mahan, A. T., *The Influence of Seapower upon History* (Boston, Mass., 1940).

Schurman, D. M., *Julian S. Corbett, 1854–1922* (London, 1981).

CHAPTER 7. THE INTERWAR PERIOD

Perhaps because of the unprecedented pace of technological change, the interwar period was exceptionally fertile in terms of the number and quality of works on military theory that it produced. It was necessary to come to terms with such unprecedented devices as the aeroplane, tank, aircraft-carrier, submarine and landing-craft; what is more, war as waged under modern industrial circumstances had to be studied and mastered.

Bialer, U., *The Shadow of the Bomber* (London, 1980).

Douhet, G., *Command of the Air* (New York, 1942).

Fuller, J. F. C., *The Reformation of War* (London, 1923).

Gat, A., *Fascist and Liberal Visions of War* (Oxford, 1989).

Liddell Hart, B. H., *The Decisive Wars of History* (London, 1929; expanded as *Strategy*, 1954).

Liddell Hart, B. H., *The Defence of Britain* (London, 1939).

Liddell Hart, B. H., *The Ghost of Napoleon* (London, 1933).

Ludendorff, E., *The Nation at War* (London, 1937).

CHAPTER 8. FROM 1945 TO THE PRESENT

Since 1945 there has been an explosion of writings on military theory. In part this was because, with major interstate wars becoming fewer and further between, soldiers had more time to write; in part, because the field was invaded by civilians who for the first time turned it into a university study. Some fine work was done on conventional war, particularly in the US and the USSR. The most significant studies were those that dealt with nuclear strategy and various types of low-intensity conflict. As of the time of writing nuclear strategy is all but dead, given that the main issues have been thrashed out decades ago and that almost everybody agrees that a nuclear war would be tantamount to suicide. Low-intensity conflict is spreading and is threatening to render all but a handful of previous military thinkers irrelevant.

Brodie, B., *The Absolute Weapon* (New York, 1946).

Griffith, S. B., *Mao Tse Tung on Guerrilla Warfare* (New York, 1961).

Freedman, L., *The Evolution of Nuclear Strategy* (New York, 1981).

Kahn, H., *On Thermonuclear War* (Princeton, NJ, 1960).

Kaufman, W. (ed.), *Military Policy and National Security* (Princeton, NJ, 1956).

Kissinger, H. A., *Nuclear Weapons and Foreign Policy* (New York, 1957).

Laqueur, W., *The Guerrilla Reader* (New York, 1977).

Lawrence, T. E., *Seven Pillars of Wisdom* (London, 1990).

Luttwak, E. N., *Strategy: the Logic of War and Peace* (Cambridge, Mass., 1986).

Orenstein, H. S., *The Evolution of Soviet Operational Art, 1927–1991* (London, 1995).

Schelling, T. C., *Arms and Influence* (New Haven, Conn., 1966).

Simpkin, R., *Race to the Swift* (London, 1985).

Till, G., *Maritime Strategy in the Nuclear Age* (London, 1982).

van Creveld, M., *The Transformation of War* (New York, 1991).

Warden, J. A., III, *The Air Campaign: Planning for Combat* (Washington DC, 1988).

INDEX

Figures in *italic* refer to captions

PICTURE CREDITS

Every effort has been made to contact the copyright holders for images reproduced in this book. The publishers would welcome any errors or omissions being brought to their attention.

ENDPAPER: *A scene from the Boxer Rebellion. Though supposedly based on guile rather than brute force, in practice Chinese warfare could be quite as bloody as its western counterpart.*